The Good Land
Farm Families Remember

This book is dedicated to the many farm families who still embrace the values and traditions fashioned by their forebears in simpler times—hard work, honesty and a strong sense of love and respect for land, family, church and country. The stories inside—accounts of farm life in the early half of this century—were gathered from hundreds of reminiscences submitted by readers of *Country, Country EXTRA, Country Woman* and *Farm & Ranch Living* magazines.

Wayne Mumford

THE GOOD LAND
Farm Families Remember

Publisher: Roy J. Reiman
Editor: Ken Wysocky
Associate Editors: Kristine Krueger, Tom Curl
Art Director: Maribeth Greinke
Design Director: Jim Sibilski
Art Associate: Gail Engeldahl
Production Assistants: Julie Wagner, Barb Czysz, Ellen Lloyd, Judy Pope
Photo Coordinator: Trudi Bellin

©1995 Reiman Publications, L.P.
5400 S. 60th St., Greendale WI 53129

Country Books
International Standard Book Number: 0-89821-146-8
Library of Congress Catalog Card Number: 95-69729
All rights reserved. Printed in the U.S.A.

For additional copies of this book or information on other Reiman
Publications books or magazines, write: Country Books, P.O. Box 990,
Greendale WI 53129

Credit card orders, call toll-free 1-800/558-1013

Photo Credits
Cover: Dick Dietrich (wheat fields and farm near Waitsburg in Washington's
Palouse region); inset, horses and mules pulling combine on the W. Rex Childers
Ranch near Almira, Washington in mid-1930's, submitted by Gordon Davis of
Sequim, Washington.
Page 3: William H. Allen Jr.
Pages 4-5: Tom Narwid (farm scene near Danby Four Corners, Vermont); Bonnie
Nance (farmer and Belgians in Indiana).

CONTENTS

Mount Burns

Rick Miller

Julie Habel

Julie Habel

Amber waves of grain pour in as pleased
Midwest grower watches (top); continuing
clockwise: Iowa farmer with two old friends;
farmer puts Farmall through its paces while
planting corn near Cottage Grove, Wisconsin;
barn in Iowa gets the brush-off from owner.

8

Heritage farm near Forestville, Minnesota (above) was founded in 1856; top right, farmer teaches grandchild the secret of good hoeing; right, old John Deere and grain drill get a workout on Whitewater, Wisconsin farm.

1

Life on the Farm

My dad, Charles Berdo, wrote this letter in 1945 when he returned to farming in Washington, Iowa. He had recently come home after serving in World War II:

"Life is really wonderful. Our 800-acre farm has been idle for 3 years, so I'm finding an unlimited number of jobs—painting barns, building fences, plowing 8-foot-tall weeds into the soil and buying livestock.

"Already the combination of bountiful nature and hard work is seen on our fair land. Fat Hampshire pigs, farrowed since my return, play happily in the fields, and 52 Hereford heifers have grown sleek and fat within a month, eating the lush fields of grass that have been untouched by livestock for 3 years.

"After 4 years in the Army, it's a real pleasure to just watch the heifers stretched out in the pastures, enjoying the warm Indian summer sun. Fortunately, my 10 horses, two tractors and all other machinery were here waiting for me. Can't express the joy at working with them again.

"It's hard to put into words, but there are so many thrills to farming. I really feel sorry for anyone who has never tried it. One of my favorite thing is driving along slowly on a wagon behind a team of horses early in the morning, when the air is nice and fresh and the dew is still on the grass alongside the lane.

"It's also nice to do the plowing and see the rich-smelling dirt, full of decaying roots and grasses, turning over and off the plow. Another fine thing to see is a barn clear full of hay right up to the top, or a crib full of corn. These are just a few of the many reasons farming gets into your blood. If you make good money, all the better.

"But once you get started, even if you don't make money, you still have the fun of farming anyway."
—*Jayne Custer*
Wayland, Iowa

Charles Berdo aboard his tractor with daughter Jayne in 1950.

I was raised on a farm, and I'm really proud of that. You seem to learn more about the value of things.

While growing up, I was a tomboy. I *had* to wear bib overalls so I could be just like my dad. As long as I can remember, I was always walking in his footsteps.

I clearly remember one day when Dad was milking "Brownie", my favorite cow—she was very gentle. He gave me a tin cup and told me I could milk on the other side.

I was only 5 years old, so when I finally filled that cup, I really thought I had done something—until, that is, I was in grade school and milking 20 cows twice a day! And that was milking by hand—there were no milking machines in those days.

No matter what we were doing, Dad made it fun. He'd say, "Let's hurry and finish this, and then I'll take you to the creek swimming." That gave us something to look forward to after the hard work was finished. —*Mazie Goodman, Dallas, Texas*

Grain from the fields wasn't just for farm animals. In my dad's granary, I used to romp barefoot in the various bins of wheat, corn and other grains. You could say this is how one gets corns on their toes! It was a soothing and relaxing time that I well remember. —*Kathryn Dieter*
Allentown, Pennsylvania

I'll never forget our neighbors, the Pearsons. I used to help them plant tobacco with their daughter, Norma Jean. We'd sit together on the back of the planter and drop the plants in by hand.

One day, when we had finished planting, Mr. Pearson told me I could drive their old Ford and wagon back up to their barnyard. I protested that I'd never driven a car before, being just 15 at the time.

"Oh, you drive your dad's tractor all the time—you can handle it," he replied. He went on ahead with his horses while I figured out how to start the car and put it in gear. Then I gave it some gas, and away I went.

Soon the car was going so fast that I couldn't collect my wits and figure out how to slow it down. I went flying around the first turn; luckily, both

the car and the wagon cleared the fences. I continued down the lane at breakneck speed—and suddenly realized I was about to pass Mr. Pearson and his horses!

I flew by and looked back at him—his eyes were as wide as saucers. How I ever cleared him, the horses and the fence, I'll *never* know. When I got to the barnyard, I took my foot off the gas pedal and the car jerked to a stop.

Mr. Pearson pulled up beside me, obviously relieved. I didn't drive that Ford again for a long time! —*Nancy Leighner, Rockford, Ohio*

The thought of preparing food for a threshing crew in the early part of this century brought qualms to even the most stouthearted farm woman, and my mother was no exception.

Mama and her helpers made mountains of mashed potatoes, enormous beef roasts or a couple dozen fryers, vegetables, salads, desserts, cream pies and gallons of iced tea or coffee. The work was more difficult when you consider that electricity and refrigeration were practically unknown commodities.

Now, Mama was an excellent cook. But one year, something strange happened. The men all trooped in from the fields, washed up at the windmill, seated themselves around our lengthened oak table and *nibbled at the food*.

Mama was aghast! She tasted the potatoes—yes, they had enough salt. She pulled the meat from the wishbone—yes, it was well-done without being dry. Why weren't they eating the meal?

She was pondering the situation when Dad

A good harvest—the reward for many months of hard work.

trudged in with a huge "Tom Watson" watermelon. "I'll put it in the cellar where it'll keep cool until supper," he said. "It's the last one from that whole wagonload I picked up this morning."

Suddenly, Mama knew why her dinner was so lightly eaten. Dad was famous for his sweet, juicy melons. And he had left a wagonload of them where the threshing crew passed by. Unable to resist, the crew had eaten their fill as they came and went with their teams and racks.

Needless to say, Dad trod very softly for several days and even complimented her on her potato pancakes—a dish he normally disliked.

—Kathryn McGaughey, Denver, Colorado

Dark clouds had been simmering on the horizon all morning, like a pan of oatmeal left on the back of a stove, with an occasional "kerplop" of muted thunder.

Busy in our world of make-believe play, my sisters and I had not noticed anything unusual about this day. In the Dust Bowl period of the early 1930's, our childhood days in western Oklahoma were pretty much the same.

In the mornings, we'd play in the front yard under the tall cottonwood tree, taking turns on a rope swing with its weathered board seat. As the shade would move, the barren ground would become so scorching hot that we'd load our toys in a little wagon and move to the grove in back of our house.

But on this late afternoon, Mom stood on the front porch and called us to come quickly. At the urgency of her voice, we dropped our playthings and raced for the front yard, barely noticing a new freshness in the air.

Rounding the corner to the front yard, we stopped, completely spellbound at the scene before us. Clouds had moved overhead, and from high in the heavens, arching down through the cottonwood, directly through our swing and ending in the hard-packed earth below, was the most dazzling rainbow we'd ever seen. We could only gaze speechless at this wonderful miracle.

Then the first plump raindrop hit the ground, and the magic spell was broken. As the icy drops began to pelt our warm, sun-browned arms and legs, we shrieked with delight and sang and danced around the yard.

The rainbow slowly began to disappear as Mom sat on the porch laughing—you could almost see the worry and tension of the past few years fading from her face. Somehow we all felt that the end of the Depression was in sight.

—Sybil Eades
Renton, Washington

Rainbow adds special drama to the Wheeler County, Nebraska landscape in this photo taken by Norman Marks of Geneva.

I remember when my grandfather first allowed me to plow the fields after school with our little Allis-Chalmers B tractor back in the 1930's.

I felt real proud—I was finally considered old enough to do it alone! But after a few times, the

Joe Henry will never forget how he broke the monotony of plowing with his family's old Allis-Chalmers tractor. This shot is from the '30's.

excitement wore off and plowing became so monotonous that I'd start to daydream. I had to do *something* to break the boredom.

Since the little tractor had a wide front end, it would usually go a long ways without ever having to touch the steering wheel; it would never jump out of the "dead" furrow.

So I got the idea of getting off the tractor and walking along behind it, just watching it go by itself. Eventually I got bold enough to just sit down and let it go; I'd allow just enough time to run and catch it, then turn it around for the trip back across the field.

I never thought anyone saw me until years later. That's when a neighbor who lived on one side of the field told me he'd seen me relieving my boredom several times. He laughed and said he'd have given anything to see me miss catching up to the tractor and watch it plow through a fence!

I wouldn't recommend that anyone else ever try this. And to this day, I don't know if this neighbor ever told my grandfather what he'd seen!

—*Joe Henry, Creston, Iowa*

I enjoyed every minute of growing up on a farm, even though there were many hard times and a lot of difficult work. As a Christian family, we were thankful for the good times and for what we had.

We lost our farm during the Depression, but soon after moved to my grandparents' farm when Grandpa passed away. That was in February of 1932. I was only 10 years old, but I still remember loading everything we had left on wagons pulled by teams of horses.

Two of the things I remember most about Grandma's farm were the sugar camp and raising potatoes. I was a tomboy and loved both these events, even though it meant hard work.

Early in the year, my dad and I would tap and fasten buckets to the maple trees. We'd load the horse-drawn sled with big drums and go from tree to tree, filling them with maple sugar.

We'd haul them to the sugar camp and start boiling the sugar down in a big vat. My job was to gather wood, keep the fire going and occasionally stir the sugar. Then we'd fill jugs with the sweet maple syrup.

In early spring, we'd plant potatoes. My grandpa had been known as "Potato Mike" around here because he had planted so many potatoes, and we carried on the tradition.

We used a horse-drawn planter. My dad would drive, and I'd sit on the back and make sure that there was a piece of potato in each section of the wheel that dropped

Collecting maple sugar was a rewarding experience for many farm families.

them into the ground. At harvesttime, we'd plow out the potatoes. Then came the backbreaking job of picking them up. We'd put them in crates, haul them to the house on a horse-drawn wagon and store them in the cellar.

We'd raise as many as *3,000 bushels* a year. It was hard work. But each of us did our part, proudly knowing that we'd helped our family through some hard times. I'll never forget—nor regret—being raised on a farm.

—*Mrs. Merlin Derringer*
Lima, Ohio

My first romance occurred in the seventh grade with a brown-eyed girl named Audrey. About 19 kids in grades one through eight attended this school in northeast Iowa, except in spring, when we older boys had to help plow, disk, drag and plant.

When summer came and farm work slackened a little, I found myself thinking about Audrey's brown eyes and long black braided hair. I asked Dad for an afternoon off to go visiting, and with a smile and a twinkle in his eyes, he agreed. Surprisingly, he even let me borrow the horse that our landlord had bought to eat the grass in the apple orchard.

Now, I knew nothing about horses, except from what I'd seen at the movies and at my Uncle Ben's. So I thought the horse would gallop me right over to Audrey's, and that I'd look pretty good riding right up to her house.

Well, this was an old horse, and he didn't like me forcing him out of retirement. I could have rolled myself faster to Audrey's. But I finally got there and rode right up to her front door, got off and knocked.

But I'd been concentrating on the horse so much that I hadn't thought about what to say to Audrey. She answered the door and looked at me with those big brown eyes, and I got all flustered. Her giggly sister was there, too, which didn't help.

The old horse broke the ice for me. See, nobody had told me what horses do after they've walked a while. Well, he did what horses do—right there on Audrey's front lawn. Of course, there was nothing more to talk about now, for sure, so I said good-bye.

But I knew I couldn't leave without cleaning up. Audrey's dad would be coming in from the fields for supper, and he wouldn't be too happy about what had happened. So I tied the old nag down at the barn, found a scoop and did what needed to be done. All the while, I could hear Audrey and her sister howling with laughter inside the house. What a way to start—and end—a romance!

—*Larry Carrier, Ottawa, Kansas*

As a child during the 1930's, I attended a one-room schoolhouse 13 miles from the nearest town. Receiving an eighth-grade diploma was the goal of all the children, and I'll never forget the day I received mine.

I was scheduled to receive it on the last day of school in the summer of 1941, along with two other students. But on this particular day, I was needed to help on the farm—a frequent occurrence for farm kids in those days.

I really wanted to be in school that day, but it was not to be. So I went out and helped Papa cut sprouts

One-room schools like this one were familiar to many farm children in the 1930's and '40's. Photo was sent by Lilly Klos of Baker, Montana.

on the back side of our field. Late in the afternoon, something caused me to look up; it was my teacher, Mr. Bateman, walking across the field with something in his hand.

He approached and handed me a magazine and told me to open it carefully. I did so, and nestled there in the middle of a copy of *Life* magazine was a piece of thick blue paper, tied with a silky blue cord and a tassel. It was my diploma!

Mr. Bateman knew how badly I wanted to be in school that last day. I have never forgotten the thoughtfulness of this wonderful man and how he cared enough to go out of his way on his long walk home to give me that diploma.

I still have it in my mother's trunk. It's one of my most prized possessions. Every time I look at it and touch the pretty tassel, my heart fills with cherished memories of Mr. Bateman and that hot summer day when I officially graduated in our field.

—*Nellie Byers, Heavener, Oklahoma*

Back in the 1950's, my husband ran a small dairy farm in Barren County, Kentucky. We were in the middle of a severe drought and badly needed rain for our hay fields and pastures.

From time to time, we'd see lightning flash in the distance at night, but the rain we so desperately needed didn't come. Then I read a piece of folklore that said if a snake was killed and hung belly-side up on a fence, it would rain before midnight.

Now, my husband considered snakes a farmer's friend, but I convinced him to try and kill just one. He happened to kill one the next Sunday and hung it on our fence. After the Sunday evening church service, we noticed lightning in the distance. I announced that it was going to rain, and some people laughed.

That snake was small, which probably explains why it didn't start raining until *after* midnight. But rain it did! Lightning flashed, thunder roared and the rain poured down—a real gully-washer.

The next day, my husband's aunt, who was visiting us from Texas, suggested that we take the snake off the fence because it had rained long enough. My husband must have felt the same way—he had already taken it off!

—*Faye Edmunds*
Hopkinsville, Kentucky

I started going to school in 1927 in a horse-drawn bus. I knew the driver well—he was my father!

Dad was more than just the bus driver. Many times he just sat on the reins and helped students with geometry and algebra. He didn't have to worry about the horses—they knew where to stop and pick up the students.

The bus had windows that we could open for relief during hot weather, and a potbellied stove up front that provided heat in winter.

In spring, the

Horseless school buses were a real novelty 50 years ago.

dirt roads were filled with deep mud. The horses would have to pull so hard going up hills that sometimes one or both would fall down. Then we kids would have to get out and walk while Dad talked to the horses awhile, then led them and the empty bus up the hill.

One evening each May, Dad would stop at a woodland area. He'd give everyone a few minutes to go pick flowers for their mothers. When he'd blow a whistle, we'd all run back to the bus.

By the time I graduated in 1939, our roads were covered with gravel and our school buses were motorized vans with wooden benches inside. But in the spring, even the new gravel roads sometimes would still get so muddy that the vans couldn't run. Then it was back to the horse-drawn buses again!

—*Flaurice Whitham, Fairfield, Iowa*

Over half a century ago, about 80 percent of farms in the United States had no electricity. When I was a child, my family lived on one of those farms in central Minnesota.

We cooked and heated with a wood-burning stove. Our refrigerator was a cool basement in the summer or a snowbank in the winter. The bathroom was an outhouse located 100 feet from the back door. Indoor light was provided by kerosene lamps, and lanterns were used outside for doing chores.

Our radio operated on batteries. Records could be played on a hand-wound phonograph. After hand-washing clothes, we pressed them with irons that were heated atop the stove.

Then, in 1935, President Franklin Roosevelt es-tablished the Rural Electrification Administration, or REA. In the late 1940's, our area of Minnesota finally received electricity. Power lines were installed along country roads and contractors were hired to wire the houses and other buildings.

One day, all was in readiness. We could hardly wait for nightfall. As the sun set, we ran excitedly through the house, switching on every light—something that probably sounds pretty wasteful in these days of energy conservation!

Then the whole family sat in our bright kitchen, looking out the window at our yard, which was illuminated by a glowing bulb sitting high atop a pole. It was a glorious day the night that our farm lit up.

—*Lucille Churchill*
Waukesha, Wisconsin

Electricity made life easier for many a farm wife, especially when it came to cleaning.

Despite all the gloom of the Great Depression, the 1930's weren't a bad time to grow up. People did a lot of improvising.

For example, we always had good beds to sleep on, even though they were straw-tick mattresses—not Beautyrests! My mom crafted those home-made mattresses out of blue striped sailor cloth sewn into big bags, then filled them with straw.

Every year after the threshing season, new straw was available. We'd open one end of the mattress, remove the old straw and launder the cloth bag with our hand-powered washing machine. Then we'd stuff the bag with new straw and place it on the bed again.

The first night on the new straw tick was like climbing on a small mountain and sleeping on prickly new-mown hay. Gradually, it became a fairly comfortable mattress—until we repeated the annual straw ritual the following year.

—*D.J. Mishler, Goshen, Indiana*

Sometimes the switch from horses to engines took a little bit of adjustment, as accompanying story points out. This Indiana farmer is using a 1953 John Deere Model B in his fields.

The switch from horses to tractors began taking place in the late 1930's.

Dad saw the need to update our farm and purchased a brand-new 1937 Model A John Deere tractor, a two-bottom plow and a two-row cultivator—all for $1,000.

I can still remember the spring day that Dad drove the tractor into our farmyard. The bright green and yellow machine was equipped with steel-rimmed wheels, which meant we had to bolt lugs to the rear wheels for traction before heading for the fields.

The tractor had a small fuel tank for gasoline that had to be turned on before starting. To start the tractor, we had to spin the flywheel by hand.

I can still hear the "putt-putt" of the so-called "Johnny Popper" as it made its first circle around the field with Dad at the controls.

Suddenly, as he neared the end of the field, I heard him yell, "Gee, haw, whoa!" But the tractor

kept on going—until Dad realized he had to grab the hand clutch to stop. Nothing drastic happened, but we laughed about the incident many times. —*Eugene Bartunek, David City, Nebraska*

During the "Dirty Thirties", my parents, younger sister and I lived on a farm in northeastern South Dakota.

Our barn had burned down years before, so my father built something unusual—a straw pile barn. He constructed a pole-and-wire framework with stalls for cows, calves and horses.

He then had the threshing crew blow straw over this framework, which formed a cozy straw barn that was warm in winter and cool in summer.

Every fall, he would have fresh straw blown over it to replace any that had sunk in or blown away. He had windows and doors put in the south side to provide some light. It reminds me now of the "earth" homes being built today!

My sister and I used to have so much fun sliding down the straw barn in winter. Since we didn't have sleds, we'd sit on scoop shovels, used to shovel grain, or pieces of cardboard.

I've never seen or heard of another barn like my Dad's. —*Phyllis Davidson, Ortley, South Dakota*

My parents were hardworking and progressive farmers, always willing to try innovative ideas.

Although we ran a dairy farm, we also kept about 300 laying hens as a second source of income. At local "poultry meetings" around 1930, someone explained that the birds would eat more feed—and thus produce more eggs—if their "day" was extended with artificial light.

Not wanting to wake up at 2 a.m. every day to turn on the chicken lights, my parents came up with a clever solution. They ran electric wires from a switch box in our back stairway out to the henhouse.

In the box was a knife-type switch to control the lights. On top of the box, they mounted a rat trap and tied a shoelace from the jaw of the trap to the switch.

They also mounted an alarm clock nearby, with a string tied from the winding key to the bait tab of the rat trap. Each night, they'd set the rat trap and alarm clock.

At 2 a.m., the alarm clock would go off, the winding key would turn and pull the string, setting off the trap. The trap would snap shut, pulling the electric switch on. The hens, supposedly, got up to begin their day while we kept sleeping.

Donald Fox, Enon Valley, Pennsylvania

Chickens provided many amusing moments on the farm —as well as good meals!

discovered that a hen does not "lay" an egg. She actually stands, strains, breathes deeply with her mouth open and finally produces an egg that pops into the nest.

Even as a child, I felt sorry for the city kids who never saw a hen drop an egg—or experienced other great lessons of farm life. —*Betty McVaigh Carrollton, Georgia*

On the farm where I grew up in Illinois, we had a two-seater outhouse—a necessity for a family of 10! In the hot summer months, the outhouse was rather cool with its dirt floor and the moon-shaped ventilation hole in the front door. Often a hen would squeeze through the front door and join me as I rested or read the Sears catalog.

The hen would go about her business, finding a corner spot, scratching around, then settling into the hollowed-out "nest". From these encounters, I

My husband tells many stories about old remedies for illnesses, but this one—from the days when his family homesteaded along Shell Creek in Platte County, Nebraska—is the best!

One day when my husband's father, Sammy, was a boy, a haying crew was working in a meadow close to the creek. All of a sudden, Sammy's dog, "Rover", set up a fierce howling. Turned out he'd been struck by a rattler and was paralyzed and dying.

Old Rover was in the way of the scythes, so a cou-

19

Good farm dogs like this bloodhound were invaluable to their owners …and playmates for the children.

ple of men carried him to the creek, where they buried him. A good farm dog is sorely missed by young and old alike, and Sammy missed him most of all.

About 2 weeks later, the grown-ups couldn't believe it when Sammy excitedly told them that Rover had come back. It was true! The only explanation they could come up with was that the mud on the creek bank had drawn the poison from the dog's body, allowing him to survive.

These days, someone would have had that mud on the market—and fast!   —*Virginia Connelly*
Moville, Iowa

One day my husband's parents decided to go to town, which was a big deal in the early 1930's since it was 20 miles away.

They checked all the animals, making sure they were locked in their pastures and pens. Then they packed a big lunch to eat in the park, got all the kids dressed in their best clothes and headed for town.

Arriving home later in the day, they noticed the pigs going in and out of the bunk house, where some food and goods were stored—including flour. They ran to the bunkhouse and, lo and behold, the pigs had gotten into the sacks of flour. The flour was all over the pigs and floating in the air, landing on everyone and anything.

The pigs looked like ghosts as the children ran after them, shouting. My husband's mother also went after the pigs, screaming and flapping her arms. The pigs grunted and oinked their way past this mad, wild woman who had lost all her flour for baking. It

was a ghostly nightmare! From then on, they made double sure the pig pen door was locked before they left the farm.

Another time, my husband, Amos, was left behind to watch the pigs as they foraged in a field. This got boring, so he decided to do his own thing and check on them later.

Hours later, there was a knock on the door. It was someone from town, complaining about a herd of pigs overtaking the town about 6 miles away.

Amos jumped out and ran to the field. The pigs had vanished. He hopped on his horse and raced into town, hoping against hope that the reported pigs weren't his. They were.

The pigs were swarming all over the streets and sidewalks. Women were flapping their aprons and men shouted and waved their hats. Children were laughing and running among the pigs while dogs barked and cats ran up trees.

Amos' heart stood still. What a mess! He weaved his horse among the pigs, trying to steer them in the right direction home. Some of them wouldn't move, so he had to jump down and twist their tails.

Runaway pigs proved to be a real headache for one family.

20

Now that's a lot of tail-twisting for a small boy, but he finally got them going on the right track. They oinked all the way home!
—Sarice Human
Hazelton, Idaho

There's a lot of discussion these days about what to pay children for an allowance—and what they should be expected to do to earn it.

But when I was growing up 50 years ago, we didn't get allowances. As kids, we just knew that when we worked together, we'd get our needs met—and some extra besides, if at all possible.

However, there *was* one way we could earn money—go through the potato field with a 1-gallon honey pail and pick off the potato bugs and their eggs. Now, potato bugs were easy to spot. Although about the size of a pencil eraser, their black- and greenish-yellow striped shells were a dead giveaway.

The eggs were just as easy to identify with their brilliant orange color, but it took a bit more effort to find them. They were hidden under the leaves, and many plants had more than one leaf containing numerous eggs.

To give you an idea of how big our field was, it would take about 1-1/2 days for 10 of us to pick all the potatoes, once they were dug up. Knowing this, you can imagine how many hours and days it took us to pick off all those eggs and bugs.

So what was the big payoff? One cent for each bug and one cent for each leaf of eggs. On a good day, we could earn up to $3 before our little backs were ready to break.

For my folks, I'm sure the $15 or so they paid

us was well worth it. See, we used potatoes to feed the hogs, as well as ourselves—sometimes for two or three meals a day. Plus, we'd sometimes sell the surplus potatoes to bring in a little extra income.

It sure was hard work. But looking back, I did enjoy getting out in the fresh air and sunshine. And the best part was the challenge of seeing how much money we could make our folks pay us!
—Carol Myers
Reedsburg, Wisconsin

During the Depression, my family depended on horses and mules both for working in the fields and transportation.

So my dad was very intrigued when my grandfather expressed interest in selling his Model T car. He and my father struck a deal—two hogs in exchange for the car.

On the way home, Daddy drove on the sandy roads for 5 miles without any difficulty. Then he reached the gate that stood at the entrance to our pasture, where there were several cows.

Daddy yelled, "Whoa! Whoa!" as he always did to the horses—and drove right through the gate. We'll never let him forget that incident.

I also remember the time we decided to sell cream from our milk cows to a dairy that made cheese in Pueblo, Colorado. Dad bought a separator and we

J.C. Allen and Son

Children played an important role in keeping a farm operating smoothly; here they search for potato bugs in 1914.

21

saved the cream until it filled a 5-gallon can.

We took the can, drove it 5 miles into town and sent it to Pueblo on a flatbed railroad car. In a few days, the can came back—with a check for $1.50.

A Model T Ford for two hogs? That was the going rate in the 1930's.

—*Eutha Hickey, El Paso, Texas*

The world has come a long way since I was a boy. We've been to the moon, silos now unload themselves and, last but not least, boys don't have to "pull strings" anymore.

If you don't know about pulling strings, then you never had a father who owned one of the first hay balers. I'm talking about the big red ones with canvas conveyor belts, a gasoline engine, and a fold-down seat welded to the chute where the hay bales came out.

That seat was located just behind an arm that pumped up and down, keeping the loose hay pushed down into a chamber where it was pressed into bales. I sat there many a day, pulling strings.

You see, the knotter—the apparatus which tied the twine that bound the bales—was so unreliable that some-

"Pulling strings" on old hay balers like this one kept farm lads alert, as story at right explains.

one had to pull every string on every bale to be sure it was tight. If the string gave way, you had to loudly yell, "Whoa! Whoa! Whoa!" until the men stacking bales on the wagon heard you. Then they, too, would join in, waving their hands, hats or hay hooks until the driver noticed.

Now, more often than not, the driver in those days was my grandpa. And he was a good driver—a very good driver. He drove and drove. No matter how many of us yelled or how much we yelled, he'd just keep right on driving.

See, Grandpa was a little hard of hearing. But it wasn't only that—who could hear much over the din of the old "F" tractor and the roar of the baler?

Finally, someone would jump off the wagon and run as fast as he could until Grandpa saw him and realized what was going on. Inevitably, he'd slam on the clutch and brake, throwing Dad off the wagon and knocking down the front row of bales.

Of course, the motor had to be shut off to fix the knotters, which meant it also had to be started again—with a hand crank. It wouldn't be proper to repeat what was said by this time out there in the hay field amid the afternoon heat and humidity. Yet, somehow we were still proud to tell the neighbors on Sunday that we had baled 12 loads that day. Why, I start to sweat just thinkin' about it!

—*Thomas Maast, Greendale, Wisconsin*

I grew up on a dairy and grain farm about 30 miles south of Chicago in the 1930's and '40's.

During that time, my mom raised chickens. She bought their feed in 50-pound cotton bags designed with colorful prints. After the bags were empty, Mom used them to make skirts and blouses for me and shirts and pajamas for my brothers.

When we'd outgrow the clothes, Grandma would cut them into squares and use the pieces to make beautiful patchwork quilts. One is now proudly displayed in our living room. It never fails to rekindle memories of my early life on the farm.

—*Marilyn Bartels Johnson, Springfield, Missouri*

While I was growing up, we lived in the tornado belt, which meant each farm had a storm cellar for protection from our often-severe weather.

Our storm cellar was built close to the house for fast entry. It was a home in the ground, about 8 feet deep and 8 feet square. It was covered with a cement dome topped with a heavy layer of dirt.

A storm cellar was meant for more than just shelter, though. It also kept our milk, cream, butter and eggs fresh and cool. Vegetables and fruits were stored there for the winter, too. The storm cellar was a very necessary part of the farm. —*Phyllis Jordan Marion, Ohio*

Once a country girl, always a country girl! I'm 92 years young and live on 10 acres that have been in my husband's family since the 1700's. My father was a farmer who grew vegetables on the river flats in Forty Fort, Pennsylvania.

As a child, I loved to go to the fields and watch them load vegetables for market. The tomatoes were put in a wagon with specially built racks that could hold baskets piled up to five high. It took four horses to pull it. The peas and beans were piled loose in wagons.

One day I decided to see where all those vegetables went. So as they loaded the wagon, I crawled under a blanket that hung down over the seat. My older brother drove the team to Scranton, unloaded the peas at the cannery—and found me under the seat!

What a surprise. He scooped me up and took me for something to eat before we made the long trip home, where my worried parents sighed with relief at the sight of me. —*Estella Risch Stecher Stroudsburg, Pennsylvania*

I recall when my brother and I were old enough to help Dad on our ranch in Colorado during the early 1920's. He raised wheat and hogs, and, of course, there were always the cattle, horses and chickens to provide plenty of chores to do all day.

I remember driving horses for Dad while cutting corn for fodder. I also recall driving the barge during harvesting, which was a dirty job with the grasshoppers spittin' their "tobacco juice", chaff falling down our necks, and the sun beating down so hard that mirages formed before our eyes.

Sometimes a storm would appear on the horizon, and, in no time, there'd be thunder and lightning. Hail was the bugaboo. It

Fast moving storm was captured by Suzette Buhr, Marshall, Wisconsin

could ruin the whole crop, so many farmers carried hail insurance.

Usually the storm clouds would appear a few weeks before the harvest, so farmers would always be looking to the sky, praying it would hold off until harvesting was complete.

At certain times of the year, the wind would blow and blow for days, stirring up dust so thick you couldn't see across the road. But then there'd also be starry nights where you could easily pick out the constellations in the big, clear expanse of sky. And if the atmosphere was just right, the aurora borealis would play across the northern sky.

Dad was a great reader. During winter, he'd bring home exciting Western books, especially those by Zane Grey. Mother would sew in the evenings, and Dad would read the books out loud to her. Of course, I heard them all—that's how I developed my love for reading.
—*Helen Webb*
Watsonville, California

Grandfather was good at predicting weather. For some reason, he was very sensitive to atmospheric changes.

I clearly remember one morning when he told us we would have to gather up the hay we'd cut the day before because it was going to rain that afternoon. He was so certain about it that my mother came out to help, and we didn't even stop for dinner until it was all in.

As we unloaded the last wagon, it began to rain. This was about 2 p.m. It rained the rest of the day and into the night.

Dale Schau (story below) took this photo in 1941 of the farm he lived on for 15 years.

Thinking of gathering hay also reminds me of how my grandmother would call us in from the field for the noon meal with her seashell. This large shell had a small opening in it the size of a trumpet mouthpiece.

About 15 to 20 minutes before mealtime, she'd go outside and blow it as loud as she could. It sounded like a foghorn!
—*Dale Schau, Millsap, Texas*

My mother often helped out in the fields, as there were only three others in our family—Dad, myself and my brother, who was a little older than me.

I especially remember one childhood incident that occurred when we were out gathering corn. My parents took me with them—baby-sitters were unheard-of in those days.

I rode in the wagon while they tossed in ears of corn. It was fun and interesting, but I was only 4 or

5 years old, and I finally grew tired. So I curled up in a corner of the wagon on a coat. The wagon started and stopped again and again as Dad spoke commands to our team of reliable horses, "Prince" and "Florie". They didn't need a driver!

I also remember the rhythmic thump of corn hitting the backboard. Soon corn was tumbling down on me, but I didn't care. I was snug and drowsy. I recall Dad getting up on the wagon and saying, "She's asleep..."

Much later, I awoke as he carried me into the house. It had been a long day.   —*Lillian Deaver*
Paris, Missouri

Electricity didn't appear on our 142-acre farm until 1946, so until then, we never knew what an ice cube was. But we still had cool drinks on those hot days when we'd help shock wheat or oats, thanks to a 2-quart aluminum kettle.

We'd slice up lemons and add some sugar, then take the potato masher and crush the lemons as much as we could. We'd fill the kettle with cold well water and place it inside a shack to keep it as cool as possible. I can still remember the taste of that lemonade—nothing could hit the spot any better.
—*Esther Ringler, Alliance, Ohio*

I'll never forget the time my father made one of my birthdays extra-special. It was harvesttime, and the sun burned down without mercy. Even the wind was hot, and Papa's shirt was wet with sweat when he came into the house from the fields.

My birthday fell during one of our busiest times—wheat harvest. Getting the wheat in was the most important thing in our lives at the time, so I never expected anything special for my birthday.

I helped Mama pick peas and lettuce for our dinner and tried to pretend it was just an ordinary day. That's why we were so surprised when Papa came in from the fields earlier than usual and said he was going into town for some ice.

My heart leapt. Ice could mean only one thing—we were going to make ice cream for my birthday! Sure enough, Papa soon returned with 50 pounds of ice wrapped in a blanket to keep it from melting. My little sister, Kathryn, and I watched Mama beat eggs until they were creamy. Then she added milk and cream and delicious-smelling vanilla.

We kids sat on the back porch and waited while Papa put a chunk of ice in a gunnysack and beat it with a hammer, crushing it into little pieces. Then Mama came out with the cream mixture and put it in the small freezer. We all took turns on the crank, adding a sprinkling of salt now and then.

When the cream began to thicken and the freezer handle was hard to move, Kathryn and I sat on it while Papa took his turn. When even he couldn't turn it, we knew the ice cream was frozen.

Mama brought out the largest cereal bowls we had and a big spoon. Papa pulled the paddle out and Kathryn and I got to lick it clean. Then Mama heaped ice cream into the bowls—nothing in

Homemade ice cream was a treat every farm child yearned for—farm dogs, too!

the whole world could have tasted better! Plenty of love and homemade ice cream made for a perfect way to celebrate a little girl's birthday. And I had both! —*Margaret Lorson, Beaverton, Oregon*

Even though we had soft water, we still stored rainwater for washing clothes when I was growing up. We used some old bathtubs to catch rain for livestock and one for our personal use.

One time after a rain, my dad decided to take a bath. He found a box of Oxydol and poured it in the rainwater tub. It made loads of suds—similar to the bubble bath scenes in the movies.

When he climbed out of the tub, he was covered with several inches of suds that he couldn't get rid of, and he had to call for Mother. She had to throw lots of cold well water over him to get the suds off. He didn't use Oxydol again! —*Dorothy Stephenson Hanna, Indiana*

Rocky Point School, located in a north-central Idaho community of stump farmers, was a place of learning, a cultural center, a theater and a Saturday night dance hall all rolled into one.

The building was perched on the highest point within a 10-mile radius. Since we farm kids didn't bathe very often, I have a sneakin' hunch the schoolhouse was built there so the wind could hit it from all four directions!

In addition to readin', writin' and 'rithmetic,

Country schools like this one were often the central gathering spot for area folks. Photo was sent by Kathryn McGaughey of Denver, Colorado.

students learned quite a few other things at Rocky Point—like pitchin' horseshoes, playin' steal sticks and seeing which kid's horse could run the fastest.

It's difficult to think about Rocky Point without remembering Miss Powell, who taught all eight grades for a number of years. She boarded with a family that lived in the bottom of a canyon about 2 miles from school, and she walked every day, wading in snow during winter and mud in spring.

Each school day, if some joker hadn't nailed the door shut or stuffed gunnysacks down the chimney, Miss Powell would kindle a fire in the big heating stove, draw a bucket of water from the cistern and do the janitorial work—along with assisting the little ones with overshoes, coats and runny noses.

Although she probably spent the evening before correcting papers and preparing for the next day, she still found the time and energy to play baseball during recess and lunch hour. And during bad weather, she'd read to us from a Zane Grey book.

Every so often, I ride my old brown horse by the spot where Rocky Point used to sit. The building is gone, but if you listen carefully, you can still hear the voices of country kids blowin' in the wind. —*Warren Smith, Lewiston, Idaho*

There's so much to remember about my childhood on a Kansas farm in the 1940's. I loved riding on an old farm horse while my daddy shucked corn by hand. He used to say that you weren't a good shucker unless you had an ear hitting the backboard in the wagon, one in the air and one being shucked—all at the same time!

We also remember trying to buy enough seed sacks of the same pattern to make a dress. With four girls, Mama was kept busy sewing. She even made long dresses so we could square dance in them; those big, burly farmers would grab us and swing us high. We loved it and would squeal with delight.

Sure, we had rough times, but there were good times, too, that made lots of memories.

—*Carol Pottorf, Oskaloosa, Kansas*

Bath time in an old washtub could be fun, as this photo from Chuck Halla, Hartford, Wisconsin, suggests.

Bath time on our farm in southwest Missouri during the 1930's came about once a month—whether we needed it or not.

With no running water, we'd have to bring the washtub into the kitchen on Friday nights. We'd fill it with warm water and the oldest of us 13 kids would go first.

We didn't change the water during the night, so it was pretty thick and soapy by the time it was the younger ones' turns. I had many brothers ahead of me, and sometimes I wasn't sure if I got cleaner or dirtier. But it had to be done, and I did my duty.

Laundry was also a big event at our house. We did it each Saturday, when we weren't in school. The first task was to carry water in pails from a spring about 200 yards down a hill from our house.

Then we'd heat the water in a 50-gallon vat set over an open fire. It usually took about an hour to get it hot enough. Then we'd fill a smaller tub with the hot water, pile in the laundry and take turns hand-scrubbing. It was very hard on the knuckles, but at least we had real clean hands once a week!

After scrubbing and rinsing, we'd wring the clothes out by hand; two of us boys would take an item and twist it in opposite directions. It worked, but sometimes it sure was hard on the clothing.

I also remember washing our hands and faces in a wash pan every day, and throwing the dirty water out the back door. I will never forget one evening when I washed my hands, shoved the door open and tossed out the water—right as Dad was coming in the door with two pails of fresh milk. He caught the water full blast—and I can't tell you what I caught... —*Alvin Mast, Chico, California*

Living on a farm always meant keeping an eye on the weather, especially since Daddy was a tad bit afraid of thunderstorms. When it "came up a cloud", as he called it, we took a path through a cotton patch and garden to my grandma's storm cellar.

The cellar had a metal bed, several chairs and stools, a bench, an old Philco

Before advanced weather forecasting, farmers had to constantly be vigilant for approaching storms.

Jeffrey L. Torretta

cabinet-style radio, several kerosene lamps and, of course, shelf after shelf of home-canned fruits and vegetables.

Trips to the cellar were like community gatherings. Usually there'd be several neighbors—Daddy managed to round up everyone!—as well as Grandma, my mom, my sisters and me. If the storm was really bad, sometimes Daddy would drive to my other grandma's house and bring her over, too.

I usually grabbed a box of paper dolls—my favorite toy—to play with. I learned to keep that box handy! While I'd play, Daddy would sit by the cellar door. Every now and then, he'd lift it up, and when he felt it was safe, everyone would go home.

I now live on a hill with a beautiful view of a valley and mountains. The old bed and radio are in my home. And sometimes, when the wind is blowing hard, the thunder is deafening and the lightning illuminates more of the sky than I care to see, I can almost hear Daddy saying, "You kids better get up and go to the cellar." Wonder whatever happened to that box of paper dolls?

—*Lynn Buchanan, Mountainburg, Arkansas*

I'll never forget how my Uncle Chester's generosity helped ease a particularly hard time for my family during the Depression.

We lived on a 160-acre farm in Kansas that was given to my mom and dad by my grandfather. Uncle Chester and Aunt Reva lived nearby on another 160-acre spread, also a gift from my grandfather.

Of course, south-central Kansas became part of the Dust Bowl in the 1930's. Our farm was just 14 miles from the Oklahoma border, and crops got poorer and poorer. By 1935, my parents were flat broke.

Their main crop was wheat. Each fall, they'd take wagonloads of wheat to the local grain elevator and have it weighed and tested.

Farmers weren't paid for the wheat until harvest was over. So to keep track of how much wheat they brought on each trip and the value of each load, the information was written on a ticket. If all was done correctly, the farmer and the elevator would have the same number of tickets and the same total dollar amount at the end of harvest.

In 1935, my dad went to the elevator after harvest to "settle up". Well, Dad had recorded 11 wagonloads of wheat and the elevator had tickets for 12. After some discussion, my father found out that Uncle Chester had purposely put one of his wagonloads of wheat in my dad's name.

Uncle Chester never told Dad about it. Of course, Dad accepted the extra money, knowing this was an easy way for Uncle Chester to help out his little sister without much fanfare.

When my mother found out about Chester's generosity, she got in the wagon and drove 2-1/2 miles

Fall harvest reminds Pauline Oliver of time her uncle quietly helped out during Dust Bowl years.

J.C. Allen and Son

to thank Uncle Chester and Aunt Reva. My cousin told me that Mom cried the whole time she was thanking them. —*Pauline Oliver, Wichita, Kansas*

On the hillside of our farm back in Pennsylvania, we had about 3 acres of land full of dandelions.

Before the flowers bloomed, while they were still tender, my mother would have us kids pick them. Then she'd dry them and put them in 5-pound sugar sacks, which she'd hang in the attic. Come winter, she'd use them to make chicken soup, which we loved.

We'd also pick dandelions after the flowers had bloomed so Mother could make wine for medicinal purposes. If we had a cold, cough or some other illness, she'd heat up some dandelion wine on the kitchen stove, add some sugar and make us drink it to cure our ills. It really worked.

When Mother died many years later, we found over 50 quart-bottles of wine down in the cellar. No one had any idea just how old this wine was, but our relatives made sure none of it went to waste.

Mother always said that God gave us dandelions to be used for food and medical purposes. I'm now 80 years old and I still think she was so right, God bless her. —*A.J. Ciarrocca, Carnegie, Pennsylvania*

During the Depression, we never had much of a variety of food, but I don't remember going hungry. We raised most of our own food, especially peas.

Actually, peas kept us from starving many times. My uncle once said, "If it comes up a storm, I'll go lie down in the pea patch, for peas have saved my life so many times."

Everyone ate lots of peas back then. During summer months, I recall getting up before the rest of the family and picking them for our lunch. I did this early before it got too hot.

We always cooked enough peas for dinner, and usually had enough left for supper. We'd cook a big piece of fat meat in the peas—no wonder we often had indigestion!

We even put the dry peas to good use, eating them during the winter months. We'd put them in a large washtub, stomp on them until the hulls would break open, then dip the peas and hulls up. As the peas would fall back into the tub, the hulls would blow away in the wind. The dry peas weren't as good as the fresh ones, but when there was nothing else to eat, they tasted pretty good. —*Verna Ray Humphrey, Palestine, Texas*

Homegrown vegetables kept dinner tables well-stocked during the Depression.

Our grocery bills were very small when we lived on a farm during the Depression. There were months when all we got at the store was Calumet baking soda, and we traded eggs for it.

We raised a large garden and canned many of the vegetables. We grew peas, green beans, turnips, radishes, lettuce, tomatoes, beets, cucumbers, cantaloupes, watermelons, peppers and carrots, plus a large patch of potatoes.

We also ate a lot of field corn, which we called "roast on ears". From our pasture, we harvested blackberries, gooseberries, walnuts and hazelnuts. We also butchered our own hogs and beef, and had chickens for fryers and eggs.

After harvesttime, we traded wheat at the grain elevator for flour, and our cows supplied us with fresh milk. We supplemented all this by hunting for rabbits and squirrels and catching fish.

Being a family of 10, we consumed a lot of food. A farm was the only place to be during the Depression! —*Melvin Housemen, Littleton, Colorado*

Homes of today are really warm compared to the one I grew up in on the farm. It was heated with a wood-burning stove, and each morning and evening, I had to fill the wood box with sawed and split wood. This wood box held eight armfuls or so of wood, and we'd empty that twice a day during the cold winter months.

We had a water reservoir that was attached to the side of the stove. It held about 15 gallons of water, and it was our job to keep the reservoir filled. The water had to be carried in from our pump outdoors. We used this water for cooking, washing clothes and bathing.

When we'd go upstairs to bed, it was always cold—very, very cold. I imagine the temperature of our bedrooms was 10 to 30 degrees all winter. We usually took a glass of water up with us just in case we got thirsty, and if we didn't drink it by midnight,

it would freeze solid by the time morning rolled around.

We always thought twice about going to the bathroom during the night. It was just too cold to get out of bed, go downstairs, then walk outside to the outhouse—which was located about half a block from the house. We developed strong kidneys in those days!

We would "bank" our house to try to make it warmer. First, we put a sheet of plastic around the foundation. Next, we piled bales of straw all around the house, then hauled horse manure and straw and covered the bales and foundation with that.

In the evenings, we'd sit in the kitchen by the stove. All unnecessary rooms were shut off to conserve heat. But we seldom got sick. I do believe all the germs just froze to death before they could make it to us. —*Curtis Nelson, Eagan, Minnesota*

I remember a time when the farmers went on strike and were dumping their milk. We had so much milk on hand and I didn't know what we'd do with it, until I got an idea. I ran the washing machine with hot water on the full cycle, then rinsed it again.

We separated the milk, put the cream in the washing machine, turned it on and made butter! I watched until it was done, then shut the machine off in time. A friend stopped by one day and was so surprised to see me wrapping butter for the freezer. We had butter and cream in the freezer for a long time after that. —*Blanche Kuester
Honesdale, Pennsylvania*

Farm couple braves winter's bite to do outdoor chores, just like reader in accompanying story.

30

Farm near Manchester, Minnesota;
inset, curious youths in rural Iowa.

31

Rows of corn under fluffy clouds (left) are in Burt County, Nebraska. Insets (left to right): checking wheat moisture content in Kansas; tractor tire makes a handy chair for Iowa farmer; farmer and granddaughter in Clinton, Wisconsin. Below, clouds float lazily over farm buildings in LaSalle County in northern Illinois.

Graceful barn near Fort Kearney, Nebraska; inset, farmer plants corn with old Farmall near Cottage Grove, Wisconsin.

Tom Layman

Frank Siteman/New England Stock Photo

Carl A. Simac

Dennis MacDonald/Unicorn Stock Photos

Julie Habel

There are always fences to fix like the one above on an Iowa farm. Continuing clockwise: airborne hay bale prepares for landing; Amish farm in Baltic, Ohio; farmer dwarfed by oxen team at fair in Topsfield, Massachusetts; serene sunset in Ohio.

35

Wooden barn and silo near Cove, Oregon (above) have picturesque setting with the Wallowa Mountains in background. Continuing clockwise: clothes hanging around in rural Iowa; wheat and radish seed fields outside Perrydale, Oregon; character-laden barn siding; farmer cradles day-old gosling.

2

J.C. Allen and Son

Animal Antics

I'm certain that animals can "talk" to each other after what my dad and I witnessed on our farm one day. See, we couldn't figure out how our dozen or so sheep kept getting out into the hay field. The sheep were given their hay and grain in bunks on one side of the lot, and on the other side was a fence to keep them out of our hay field.

We checked the fence and there was no way the sheep could get through it. So one morning, my dad and I went out extra early and hid behind the barn. We couldn't believe what we saw.

One of our mules was standing by the fence in the hay field. And as we watched, the sheep would walk up to him, one at a time, let him pick them up by the back of their necks with his teeth and lift them over the fence. When he had them all over, he went back to his feed.

At first, Dad was really upset. But then we got to laughing because it was so unbelievable. I *still* laugh whenever I see mules and sheep together!

—*Ellen Blair, Belton, Texas*

We had an unusual cow named "Babe" in our herd of Guernseys on our Blue Star Dairy near Coeur d'Alene, Idaho. Babe was the best milker in the herd, as well as a good mother. She was so good, in fact, we had problems with her wanting to mother every calf born on the place.

One evening at milking time, my husband noted that Babe's milk production was down, although she seemed perfectly healthy. Several days passed, and this milk shortage continued. It was a real mystery. Then, one afternoon while Grandpa was working in the orchard, he noticed Babe standing next to the calf pens. He went over to the pen and immediately realized what was going on.

Old Babe was standing just as close as she could to the fence, allowing the calves to reach through and nurse. Our mystery was solved, but the situation caused us to change the fences so the boards were closer together.

For years after that, we had to watch Babe whenever she was in a herd with new calves. If we didn't, she'd soon sidle up to the pen where the baby calves were and, if possible, let them nurse. She wanted to be a mother, not just a good dairy milk cow.

—*Irene Bennett Dunn, Hope, Idaho*

Our horse, "Prince", sure lived up to his name. He was always cooperative and easygoing—a real "prince" of a horse!

For example, I had a hard time getting on him, so I'd take an ear of corn and put it on the ground in front of him. When he'd lean down to eat it, I'd sit on his neck, and when he was finished eating, he'd raise his head and I'd slide down onto his back.

I was only 7 or 8 years old at the time, so

This horse must have been as patient as "Prince" in story at left!

when my parents found out how I got on Prince, they made me walk him in from the pasture.

Once four town kids and I were riding him when the girl in back started slipping off. Pretty soon we'd all fallen off, and Prince just stood there and waited for all of us to get up.

I got my own horse at age 10. She lived to be 33 years old and said good-bye to me before she died. When I came into her stall to check on her, she raised her head, whinnied, laid her head down and was gone. It was a very sad day. —*Eileen Lehman*
Orrville, Ohio

Back in my preschool days, a stray dog came into my life. A bit shaggy, thin and anxious to please, he easily won the sympathies of my mother and older sisters.

Having never seen such a big dog up close, I warmed up to him more gradually. He came to stay. We named him "Collie", because that's what he looked like, though now we know he was a Border collie-sheltie mix.

Collie was a faithful friend and wonderful farm dog. Someone had taught him about herding cattle—or else he learned very quickly. He became an essential helper, knowing just what was expected of him whenever we'd round up the eight or so milking cows and walk them out of the pasture gate, down a lane to the gravel road, across a bridge and down another lane leading into the milking barn.

He was so good at it that we eventually let him "walk the cows" by himself, twice a day. Of course, the cows knew what was expected of them, too.

They were all quite tame; we knew their personalities, and they knew their names. Most were Holsteins, Dad's type of milk cow. Once in a while, "Trijntje", an Ayrshire that was Mom's pet, would get a bee in her bonnet and act up by giving Collie and us kids a run for it. Near the garden, for example.

Now, I must mention that Trijntje had a magnificent long tail. If hair is a woman's crowning glory, her tail was hers. That's why I'll never forget the time I saw Trijntje pause near the sweet corn just once too often.

Collie strode up to her and grabbed a good mouthful of tail, them braced himself. She let out a startled bawl, then headed down the road, over the bridge and toward the pasture—with Collie still firmly attached to her outstretched tail.

Collie kept his legs braced—he didn't want to give an inch. She dragged him about a mile—or at least that's how far it was when Mom retold the story many, many times. She would laugh 'til she cried as she envisioned the sight again in her later years.

It's a wonderful memory for me, too. When I got older, my chores got tougher. No more watching Collie herd cows from the safety of Mom's side. Fences, feedlots and pastures were put up around the barn. But those early years, when hard work was occasionally interspersed with the hilarious, are the precious sights and sounds in my mind.

—*Jan Westendorp, Martin, Michigan*

I remember a very special animal on our farm in north-central Wisconsin during the 1930's. Our sow had a large litter of piglets and was unable to

"Checker", a faithful Border collie, lives in Balsam Lake, Wisconsin.

Larry T. Dale

care for two of them. Since it was early in March—still pretty cold in Wisconsin—we brought the piglets into the house and kept them in a straw-filled box in a corner behind our woodburning potbellied stove.

My mother fed them with cow's milk in a baby bottle. One piglet didn't make it, but the other one did; we named her "Orphan Annie". When spring arrived, Annie found herself in a small pen in the corner of the cow barn; she was never put in a pen with the other pigs.

Annie became quite a pet. During the day, she followed us about the farm, and in the evenings, she found her own way to her place in the barn. She liked to have her ears and chin scratched and would come whenever we called her.

She'd never stray from the farm. A few times, when the other pigs broke out of their pen, she would come to the house or wherever we happened to be and "oink" away to let us know.

Annie eventually became old and very fat, and because it was the Depression, she was sold. We missed her. I've never forgotten how special she was to us.

—*Lucille Schwark, Friendship, Wisconsin*

We had one cow I'll never forget—she was rather cantankerous. One day, instead of using the nearby barn door to get outside, she decided to try the window and got stuck.

We kids thought it was a funny sight and all ran for our cameras, laughing. She just looked at us as if to say, "What are *you* looking at? It's *not* funny!"

My dad didn't think it was funny, either. He's a pa-tient man, but that cow tested him to his limit that day. It wasn't pleasant for him or the cow. I'm not sure what stunts she tried after that day—maybe fence-jumping or moon-jumping. But she never tried jumping through a barn window again!
—*LeAnn Gossen
Corn, Oklahoma*

When it comes to cows, expect the unexpected, as story at left proves.

My father had a strawberry roan-colored horse, "Old Jim", who had outlived his usefulness by many years. About 10 miles from our farm there lived a knacker who took and disposed of such animals.

At my father's request, he came one day for Old Jim. He tied Old Jim to the back of his wagon and took him away. The next morning, Jim stood with his head over the barnyard gate waiting for his breakfast!

It was a miracle how he found his way home, as the roads were drifted from fence to fence with snowbanks. But Old Jim had gone through fields and over stone wall fences—my father tracked his route. He was like a homing pigeon.
—*Mae Hardin, Sussex, New Jersey*

As a little girl, I sang to our cows. They hated it, but still watched and listened as I stood in the loft and wailed rafter-high notes that fell heavy on their twitching ears. I knew what they were thinking; let's just say their actions spoke louder than words. See, "Tiny", our milker, tried to get even once by goring me. She used her new calf as an excuse, but we both knew she tried pinning me to the stall door because of my high pitches...and we weren't talking about hay.

There was a black bull, too, who gave me a look I've seen in years since then on the faces of some men as they, too, "pawed the ground" during one of my not-so-melodious outbursts.

Our sheep fared worse than the cows, as by evening, they were locked tight inside their long stall for the night and couldn't leave. Strangely, the cows could leave, but didn't. It must have been the combination of wanting their supper, which lay in the hallway of the barn below me, and curiosity at the sounds coming from a "creature" such as I.

With my arms gesturing and body swaying, my singing must've sounded something like one of them at calving time! Anyway, they weren't as "cowardly" as a lot of people I know who just turn the radio up full blast every time I sing. —*Sandi Keaton Monticello, Kentucky*

Cows proved they missed their owners by producing less milk in their absence.

with you girls?" They all mooed and then became quiet and started eating.

The cows also gave less milk during the evening milking. In fact, when the fellow who took our milk to the creamery was unloading ours the next morning, he asked my husband if he'd lost some cans. He just explained that we weren't there for the evening milking and the cows had held back.

—*Blanche Kuester, Honesdale, Pennsylvania*

Our miniature horse, "Kermit", sure saved the day for us when our farm on the Red River flooded. When the floodwaters rose, we were contract-grazing over 300 calves for a large company. All but about 12 acres of our farm was under 8 feet of water, so the owners decided to send trucks to pick up their cattle.

We set up a temporary holding pen, alleyway and loading chute in the middle of the highway, and along with many friends and neighbors, my husband began to gather the calves. They brought them

When we weren't around, our dairy cows really missed us. For instance, one day in 1950, my husband and I went to visit some friends. We did the morning chores and arranged for our sons and some relatives to take care of the evening chores.

When we came home that night, we heard quite a commotion coming from the cows in the barn. My husband ran in and asked the cows, "What's wrong

to the holding pen and I counted them as they were loaded.

I had counted all but about 70 head when my husband rode up and said, "That's it! There are no more calves." At that point my nerves were totally frazzled, and I broke down and began to cry. On top of everything else, how in the world would we be able to pay for 70 head of cattle?

Just then I heard a whinny, and when I looked up, Kermit was galloping out of a wooded area, followed by each and every one of those missing calves! We still have Kermit. He earned a home for life!

—*Margie Brown, Shreveport, Louisiana*

We raised Hereford cattle, which we call "whitefaced" here in Oklahoma. We bought a beautiful cow at an auction. But she was so wild that we had a hard time getting near her or herding her into the barn or any of the pens.

One day as I was standing outside a small pen at the end of the barn, that wild cow came in, looked at me, lolled out that long tongue of hers and gave me a swipe from chin to forehead. I figured that because my hair was snow-white, she looked at me and thought, "Hey, she's a whiteface, too, so I'm going to be friendly!"

—*Fern Folk*
Pryor, Oklahoma

Have you ever seen little lambs at play? They're the most appealing of any animals—they run, caper and jump over each other and their mothers.

One winter, one of our ewes had triplets. She could care for only two of them, and that's how we got "Billy Buster". We fed him from a bottle until he could eat by himself.

He was a round, woolly little fellow with a black face, and oh, how we loved him. When we left for school in the mornings, Mother had to hold him or he'd have followed us to school like Mary's little lamb.

Sometimes we'd hitch Billy Buster to a little cart, but the only way we could get him to pull it was to have one of us walk in front of him with a pail of oats.

We liked to get on our knees and butt heads with him. He thought that was fun, too, but after he got bigger, it backfired. We had a croquet set that furnished us with many hours of entertainment in the summer. Billy Buster liked to play, too, and if we didn't watch him, he'd butt us.

But cute little lambs become big awkward sheep; we knew it couldn't be otherwise. So one sad day, a truck came to take Billy Buster to market. We all stood in the driveway and waved good-bye. Even Mother shed a few tears.

—*Rachael McKeag*
Seattle, Washington

One day my brother, Randy, and I went to our grandparents' 40-acre farm near Huntsville, Missouri to help them load a pig named "Pokey".

Grandpa backed up the truck to the loading ramp and was holding the gate open, waiting for my

Barnyard animals provided hours of entertainment for kids on the farm

grandma, brother and me to "run" the pig in. Grandma called Pokey (all their animals had names and came when Grandma called!), and he came trotting up, probably expecting to be fed.

Grandma tried to get him to follow her, but he wanted no part of it. So Randy, Grandma and I tried herding him into the truck, but each time we would get close to the ramp, Pokey would bolt away.

After several failed attempts, we almost had him in the chute when he turned around completely and bolted straight at Grandma. Pokey ran right between her legs and threw her up in the air. She landed right on a "cow patty"!

Now, Grandma was usually gentle with all the animals. But that pig had made her hoppin' mad. She picked up a nearby board and smacked that pig square on the snout. Then, after she swatted him a couple of times on the rump, he walked right up the ramp and into the truck.

After the pig was loaded and we knew Grandma was all right, my brother and I couldn't help laughing—along with Grandma and Grandpa. This happened sometime in the mid-1960's, and I'd give *anything* to have a video recording that captured the expression on Grandma's face when she realized where she had landed. It's a sight I will never forget!
—*Audrey Chaney, Linn Creek, Missouri*

Stubborn pig gave Audrey Chaney's Grandma all she could handle.

Kathy M. Toris

We milked a large herd of Jerseys by hand, and each member of the family had certain cows to milk. One of the smartest animals I remember was a Jersey my dad gave me as a calf.

We had a barn with stanchions, but in summer, when the weather was hot, we would milk all the cows we could out in the lot. I could go out in the lot with a milk pail and sit down on a stool, and my cow would come to be milked. She would walk up beside me with her leg back so all I had to do was start milking.

Sometimes, I would tease her and start milking another cow first. She would fight the other cow away and then walk up to be milked herself. Or I wouldn't start milking right away, and she'd turn her head and gently nudge me.

If I was away threshing or doing something else at milking time, she'd be left until last. If I still wasn't there, they'd put her in a stanchion, but she wouldn't give them any milk. When I got home, I would walk through the barn door and she would bawl to me.

I taught some of our colts different tricks, but that cow taught herself!
—*Harley Allen*
Roseville, Illinois

My family had a cow named "Dummy" who was never where she was supposed to be. She had a bad habit of opening any gate or bin with her horns or tongue.

She wouldn't even give her milk like other cows; she'd start, then quit. She did this all the time. It would take us 30 minutes to milk her.

Then there was "Season", the horse. He would always stop by a gate, even while going at a full gallop. He'd even stop at fence sections that *used* to be gates. We couldn't figure out how he knew they used to be gates.

We also had a dog named "Fido" who was revered by my oldest brother, Bob. You see, rattlesnakes abounded on our ranch. And one day, Fido dashed out of the yard and grabbed Bob by the trousers and pulled him over backward. It was then that we saw a huge rattler in Bob's path.

—*Lilly Klos*
Baker, Montana

Old-timers in our area will never forget the time our 1,500-pound Hereford bull climbed into the barn loft to eat our tasty lespedeza hay.

We had a large loft and always put up loose lespedeza hay. The loft had openings over the mangers to make it easy to feed hay to the cows. And to feed our horses and mules, we threw hay down a large stairway and into a hall, then carried it from there to the horse and mule stalls.

On this particular day, Daddy went to the barn before supper to feed the horses and cows. Because the hay was dry, the lespedeza leaves fell off easily. Therefore, as the hay was thrown down the stairway, leaves piled up on every step. Daddy figured he'd take care of that by leaving the door to the stairs open and letting the cows in the barn eat the hay leaves off the steps that they could reach.

Well, our big Hereford bull found the leaves first and started to feast on the delicious leaves. As he ate the leaves off one step, he'd move up to another. Step by step, he ate his way into the barn loft.

When Daddy returned to the barn after supper to finish feeding, he found the bull in the hayloft, still eating his choice of the lespedeza hay. Daddy ran back to the house to tell Mama, who got on the telephone and started calling neighbors for help. It seemed like our barn lot was full of neighbors' cars and trucks in a matter of minutes.

We were fortunate that the bull wasn't mean. After snapping a rope to the ring in his nose and running the rope through a pulley attached to a wall downstairs, several men got behind him and pushed him toward the stairway. He eventually came down the same way he went up—with some encouragement.

For several weeks, the talk of the community was about Burr Hight's bull getting into his hayloft!

—*Russell Hight*
Jackson, Tennessee

When I was growing up on a farm in central Indiana in the 1930's, my brother and I wanted a puppy like all the other neighbor kids had. But for some reason, our daddy thought that dogs had no place on a farm.

Dad said he didn't want a dog chasing cows, chickens or cars on the road, like he'd seen some neighborhood dogs do. Plus, I think he knew that he or Mother would probably end up taking care of the puppy.

Well, as luck would have it, Daddy's favorite sister from Indianapolis came to visit one spring day and brought along a little toy collie puppy. She was so cute—we loved her instantly. We didn't say much or beg to keep her, but surprisingly, the puppy was left at the farm. Daddy just wouldn't do any-

A bull similar to this one had lofty expectations about eating dinner on the Hight family farm.

Puppy named "Skippy" proved his worth to Lucille Stamper's doubting dad.

thing to displease his sister.

We named the puppy "Skippy". She got lots of tender loving care from me, my brother and my mother. But Daddy just could not come around to accepting Skippy into our farm family.

Years passed, and we had lots of fun with Skippy. We taught her a few tricks and took good care of her. She was loved by all of us—except Daddy.

One hot summer night, Skippy was barking up a storm, and she just wouldn't be quiet. Daddy finally got up to see what the problem was and discovered that a young calf had fallen in an old well out in the pasture, not far from our back porch.

The cows had rubbed and pushed on the old fence around the well—probably to scratch themselves—and part of the old fence had broken. The small calf got through the fence and fell into the well because the old wooden platform had rotted.

Daddy hurried out, and he and my brother were able to get a rope around the calf and pull it out of the well. After that, Skippy held a more important place in my daddy's eyes.
—*Lucille Stamper*
Danville, Indiana

When I was growing up, we had a pony named "Lightning". Now, with nine of us children and often a few cousins or neighbors around, it was not an easy job for one pony to carry all of us.

But he seemed to sense who was on his back; if it were an older child, he'd run fast, but if it were a smaller one—even with an older one on, too— he'd plod along like an old plow horse.

Lightning was usually very agreeable. But when he'd get tired, no one could get on him, no matter what. Finally, we'd give up, and after he rested, he was a willing partner again.

He hated storms, and if we were riding and one came up, he headed for the barn. Nothing could stop him. And when he got to the barn, he would stop politely at the stable door for us to get off and remove the saddle. Daddy used to say he had more sense then we did—he always knew when to come home.
—*Ruby Neese, Liberty, North Carolina*

I'll never forget one time when my father decided to butcher a pig. The pig was about half grown or more, and very well rounded out. It had been roaming the premises without being penned up, and was rather shy.

We first attempted to get the pig into some pen or corner, but it resisted every effort. As soon as it realized it was cornered, it would charge the human blockade and run off again. So we just decided to try to tire the pig out.

Each of us chased him in hopes that he'd become exhausted enough to stand still so we could lasso him. However, this pig possessed a remarkable degree of endurance, and soon all of us kids were standing around catching our breaths.

Finally, the hired man took after the pig in a hot chase about the yard. The pig ran around the house to the right, then headed downhill toward the public road. All at once, the hired man got close enough to attempt a well-timed grab for the fleeing pig.

But as luck would have it, just as the hired man reached for the pig's hind leg, a cotton twilled clothesline that was strung between two trees caught him just under the chin.

He somersaulted in the air, making a complete turn—or so all the witnesses believed. He fell to the ground on his back, the breath knocked out of him.

Despite the fact that it could have been a serious injury, all the witnesses to the "gymnastics" were so convulsed with laughter that the victim's plight was temporarily forgotten.

I cannot recall the final outcome of the butchering plans, but I really doubt that any further attempts were made that day. We later conjectured that the fact the clothesline broke was what had

There's always one pig that has to be a little different, as story proves.

saved the hired man from suffering a dislocation—or worse!
—*J.G. Maughan*
Morris, Minnesota

As a farm girl, I had a registered Holstein heifer for a 4-H project, and later had her heifer, too. When the herd had to be auctioned for economic reasons, the auctioneer built my cow up as the only registered one in the sale.

I cried like a baby during the sale, which probably helped the price! Years later, my new husband took a job as a farmhand. After we moved in, the farm owner came to me and asked my maiden name. It turned out he had bought my 4-H heifer and she was still in his herd! Was I ever glad to see her!
—*P.A. Miller, Danbury, Connecticut*

I was born and grew up in a country town where nearly every family had a cow and a pen of chickens. The cow provided us with fresh milk, and the chickens—well, we sometimes had them for dinner, and Mother sold any extra eggs or exchanged them for groceries at the store.

Our chickens had the run of the yard. One day my little brother was playing with a long stick and accidentally hurt a little chick. I cuddled it in my hands and took it in the house to Mother. Its leg was hurt, and she said it would probably die.

I was about 8 at the time. Mother got a toothpick, broke it in two and helped me fashion a splint and bandage the chick's leg. Then I carefully wrapped

Carol Ottoson of Portland, Oregon poses with her two cows, "Patsy" (left) and "Lizzie", in 1947.

47

Roosters like this one became the beloved pets of many a farm child. Photo from Hearl Wilkins, Hollywood, Florida.

it in a soft cloth and placed it in a shoe box.

He didn't die. He limped for a while, but he grew up to be a big Red Rock rooster—and the neighborhood pet. "Red" followed us all over and he loved having us pick him up and carry him around. Sometimes we'd tuck his head under his wing, then gently stroke his neck until he'd fall sleep.

He roosted in a big cardboard box under the back step until it snowed. Then Mother put him in the coop with the rest of the chickens. I objected, but Mother explained that Red needed to be in the coop where the other chickens could help keep him warm.

As the winter went by, we sort of forgot about Red until one Sunday the next spring. We were having chicken for dinner when someone commented on the chicken's funny hip bone. We all realized immediately which chicken we were eating.

We lost our appetites and left the table. Father felt bad, too. He said he never thought about Red; he just grabbed the chicken that was the easiest to catch.

—*Barbara Smith, Draper, Utah*

I didn't have a little lamb while growing up on our Iowa farm, but I *did* have a faithful dog named "Shep" that followed me every day to our country school in Plymouth County.

Shep came as a tiny, lovable ball of fur when I was 6 and my little brother, Sam, was 4. Oh, how we loved that little brown puppy! She was half collie and half German shepherd, and she worshiped the ground we walked on.

My father had hoped she would be a cattle dog one day. She was okay with the cattle, but her whole life was spent in loving and protecting us and seeing that we got to school safely.

When I started school, Shep started also. We walked 1-1/2 miles to school across fields; it was a 3-mile trip if we used the dirt road. Shep always trotted beside us. She would take time to scare up rabbits, squirrels, gophers and even an occasional coyote or fox. Then she would return to trot beside us for a while.

Most times, Shep would stay at school all day. She'd romp with us at recess, chasing balls and running with us as we raced. In winter, she'd run beside us as we coasted on sleds down a long hill by the school. Usually she would curl up in a snowbank, and occasionally, when it was very cold, the teacher would even let her stay in the school's enclosed porch, where we kept our tin pails and the big crockery jug of water.

As she got older, she would go home on bitter cold days until my father would say, "Shep, time to go get the children." Then she would come to get us. She was always waiting for us at the door, wagging her tail. She was never late.

"Shep" and Mary Vogt's brother, Sam, enjoy a moment of playtime on their family's farm.

She would chase any stray animals—and sometimes people—out of the way of her children. She was our guardian and best friend in the world.

When I was very young, I took all my troubles to Shep. I would pet her as I talked to her. She would look at me with those big brown eyes, and listen and console me.

When I started high school, which was in a different direction, Shep was confused temporarily. But she soon continued on to the country school with my younger brother. When my brother started going to high school a few years later, she learned to walk with him to the bus half a mile away and then go home.

She continued to be a faithful loving friend all the days of her life.   —*Mary Vogt, Lincoln, Nebraska*

The best dog we ever had was a solid black hound named "George" who knew without a doubt that my dad was his master. George accompanied him just about everywhere.

We lived in a rural area, and my parents owned and operated a small country store about a quarter mile from our house. My dad walked to the store each morning and worked until my mother took over at noon. Dad would go home and do odd jobs around the house, then return in the evening to help Mom close the store. George went with Dad on every trip between the house and store.

When Dad suffered a stroke and was confined to bed, George began sleeping on the porch on a rug Mom placed next to the door. George never offered to go inside the house.

But one morning, the first time the door opened, George rushed inside and went straight to Dad's bed. He laid down on the hardwood floor under the bed and stayed there all day. Dad died at 8:05 that evening; it was as if George knew the end was near.

Dad was buried in a little cemetery on a hillside about a quarter mile from our house. Every day, George would take a shortcut across the field and go to the cemetery, where he'd lie on Dad's grave.

One day, George didn't return. We looked all over and asked everyone we knew if they'd seen him. Several days later, a man told us he'd seen a dead dog in the field. Sure enough, it was George, lying on the trail he'd made between our house and the cemetery. To his last day, George was faithful to his master.   —*Lucy Helton, Cawood, Kentucky*

Money was scarce on our West Virginia farm in the 1930's, so my father decided to raise a flock of chickens. He went to a hatchery and came home with 200 baby chicks.

It became my job to clean out the brooder house as the chicks got older, as well as feed them and provide fresh straw and water. By late summer, they were almost grown.

One young rooster, who already had grown inch-long spurs, thought he was a real hotshot and began challenging my mother when she did the evening feeding. He'd sidle up to her, making strange sounds and attempting to spur her around the ankles. He did this stunt a few times, becoming increasingly bolder each time.

Finally, one evening, he flapped his wings furiously and attacked

Hard to believe, but sometimes these cute little chicks turned out to be mean roosters with sharp spurs.

Mother, striking her on the lower leg. She came into the house, her leg bleeding and temper flaring. "That young rooster has just struck his last blow," she said.

It took quite a while for her anger to cool. And as you might guess, we had a delicious fried chicken dinner the next evening! —*Mary Clay*
Palm Coast, Florida

Our first and only part-Angus calf was named "Angie". Her mother was a Holstein dairy cow and her father was a registered Angus bull. We fell in love with her at once and decided to raise her. She produced numerous little black calves, which became the start of our beef herd.

Angie was a smart cow and very tame. When we turned the dairy cows out for exercise so we could clean the barns, we could count on her walking right in and cleaning up any leftovers in the mangers.

She could open gates and doors with her educated nose. One day I found her in the grain bin; she

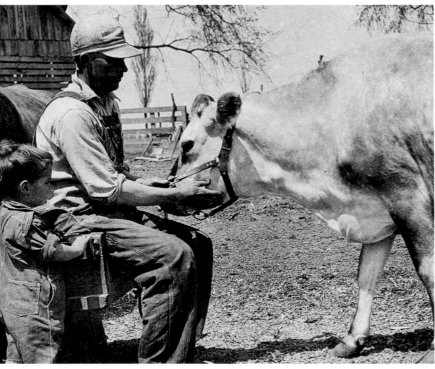

Like "Angie", the Staebler family's cow, this cow was obviously a much-loved part of this farm family.

had opened both sliding doors—one which had been fastened with a hook!

Another time, I heard her bawling and found her trapped under an old side-delivery hay rake. To reach a succulent clump of grass, she'd crawled under a brace on the rake, then stood up. She couldn't move forward and couldn't get her rump down to back out. It didn't bother her a bit; she knew she could depend on me to get her out.

On one hot summer day, she unhooked the door on the well house, went in and laid down on the planks covering the well pit. I found her contentedly chewing her cud. I told her to get out, but as she got up, a plank broke, leaving her hind legs hanging in the well pit. She didn't struggle at all; she just looked up at me and waited, confident that I would take care of things.

After encouraging her to remain quiet, I finally shoved a four-by-four timber under her belly and told her to try and get up. She managed to squirm forward and was able to crawl out the front door. Then she shook herself, gave me a self-satisfied smirk and ambled back through the gate and into the barnyard.

Angie was quite a clown, providing us with many hours of amusement and many offspring. She lived to a ripe old age and was buried, tearfully, here on the farm. —*Donald Staebler, Ann Arbor, Michigan*

We raised our three children on a small 10-acre farm near the town of Snohomish in Washington. We had the usual assortment of farm animals: a milk cow, several herd of Hereford beef cattle, pigs, chickens, ducks, rabbits, cats and, of course, our dog, "Cindy". Cindy was more than a dog—she was family, too! Half-lab and half-springer spaniel, she never ceased to amaze me.

One day some friends and their small children were over to visit. The children became fascinated by a banty hen and her brood of chicks, and they started trying to catch the chicks.

In the melee, one chick got separated from its mother and ended up in a patch of briars and stinging nettles. Cindy was very concerned; she kept looking toward the sound of the frantically cheeping chick, then toward the mama hen and then up at me.

Wondering what she would do, I said, "Go get it, Cindy!" That was all she needed. Off into the briars she went, emerging in a few seconds with the chick tucked safely in her mouth.

After dropping it into my waiting hands and seeing it placed back with its mother, Cindy stood there, wagging her tail and grinning—and yes, I do mean grinning—satisfied that all was well once again on the farm.
                              —Shirley Van Mechelen
                                    Everett, Washington

Some folks in the village near our farm had a Jersey cow named "Daisy". As the only animal they had, she was spoiled rotten. Eventually they decided they couldn't keep her anymore, and asked if we'd add her to our herd of Jerseys. We agreed.

Daisy soon let us know that she was going to rule the roost. She *had* to be the first cow milked, the *first* one let out to pasture and the *last* one to come

in. It took our dog, "Tamzy", several days to realize that this cow was different; it sure looked funny to see Tamzy herding the cows in with Daisy trotting along behind.

Whenever we had company, we'd invite them to the barn for milking time. Then we'd pretend we were going to start milking another cow first. Daisy would jump up and down and bellow until we milked her. Everything went smoothly as long as we treated Daisy like royalty!
                              —Theodore Herrick
                                    Zephyrhills, Florida

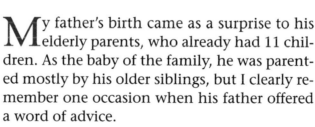

My father's birth came as a surprise to his elderly parents, who already had 11 children. As the baby of the family, he was parented mostly by his older siblings, but I clearly remember one occasion when his father offered a word of advice.

Dad was only a small boy, but already mischievous enough to enjoy teasing their large turkey gobbler. My grandfather suggested that Dad leave the turkey alone, but this advice fell on deaf ears. One day, as the old man was watching, the turkey batted the little boy with his large wing.

Then it was my grandfather's turn to laugh. For weeks afterward, when my dad had to use the outhouse, he would wait patiently by the back door of the house until the turkey walked to the front of the house. He'd race to the outhouse, then wait patiently again until it was safe to sprint back to the house!
                              —Kris-Ann Moyer
                                    Littleton, Colorado

Turkeys like this one could make something like a routine trip to the outhouse a real adventure!

Cows at Trout Acres Farm near Montgomery, Vermont are curious
(left). This page, clockwise from upper right: gaggle of geese; woman
with piglet in Pleasant Hill, Illinois; mules snacking on Kentucky
bluegrass; playful lambs; colt among mares in Trail, Minnesota.

Lynn M. Stone

Gail Denham

Bonnie Nance

Anthony Beaveson; inset: Larry T. Dake

Peter Burian

Four cats squeeze in for purr-fect pose for James Phillipp of Eden Valley, Minnesota (left); lower left, goat hams it up for camera; below, cows feast on fresh hay; right, pigs head for some fresh air.

Londie Padelsky; inset, Julie Habel

Cow plays "peekaboo" next to barn in Iowa (far left); at left, colorful chicken preens for photographer Sheri Stevens, Dothan, Alabama; below, friendly horses on Pocatello, Idaho farm of Norman Rogers.

Julie Habel

Gail Denham

Bonnie Nance

J.C. Allen and Son

Horses get first-class service from young Iowa farmhand (above). This page, continuing clockwise: lamb gets playful hug; powerful Belgians strain mightily against their load; contented pigs at feeding time. Opposite page: Holsteins find choice grazing near Black Earth, Wisconsin; inset, thirsty goslings eye a drink.

Doin' Chores

While growing up on our small 10-acre farm in northeastern Illinois, I learned that milking the goats we raised for milk and meat could be sheer poetry—literally!

You see, milking the goats became my job by the time I was 9 years old. But I disliked milking so much that I memorized poetry while doing it to keep my mind off the job.

I copied poems from books so I could carry them to the barn unnoticed. I have no idea how many poems I memorized, but there were many, including quotations from Shakespeare, portions of *The Song of Hiawatha*, and poems by Whittier, Longfellow, Poe, Browning, Burns, Wordsworth, Keats, Shelley, Whitman, Byron, Stevenson, Tennyson, Emerson, Holmes, Lanier, Kipling, Lowell and more.

Many of these poems I still can recite, although I am now 83 years old. It was a good experience for me, although I didn't think so at the time!

—*Mary Gardener, Forest Park, Illinois*

I was raised on a small farm by today's standards. I was the eldest of three children, and since we had dairy cows, turkeys and chickens, there were plenty of chores for all of us.

I started milking cows when I was 6 years old, and even had my own cow, "Shirley", named after Shirley Temple. I soon mastered the art of milking and helped with this chore day and night.

As I grew older, I became Dad's "right-hand man". In addition to milking, I'd help bed the barn with sweet-smelling straw, clean the milk parlor and feed the calves.

I also shocked wheat, tended the garden, picked berries and gathered corncobs and wood for the morning fire. You name it, I did it!

I really enjoyed the time I spent working with my dad; we were very close. He was a true farmer—a man at one with the land—and it showed in his smile and love of nature.

The country still gives me peace and contentment. Instead of tending cows, I feed my dogs, cats and the birds. I also enjoy the hills, sunrises and sunsets on my 16-acre farm, knowing the serenity of country living. Those farm chores of long ago taught me responsibility, love for animals and an awareness of the beauty around me. In essence, it made me, me.   —*Velma McCall, Stockdale, Ohio*

Like girl in story, this farm girl enjoyed helping Dad with chores.

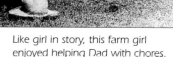

Our daily chores included sawing and chopping wood, bringing in coal, feeding and watering the animals, milking, separating the milk, gathering eggs and cleaning the stables.

Most chores weren't much fun. But some—like

mowing hay and plowing—were pleasant. To this day, I get great joy watching the soil turn over while plowing. It fascinates me.

It's the same thing when I watch hay fall as it's cut. And the smell of newly mown hay is really wonderful.   —*Eugene Barker, American Fork, Utah*

Like most farm children, we were all assigned chores—and I never remember any of us objecting.

We lived in a large house that was heated with wood stoves and fireplaces. That meant lots of wood had to be carried in every day.

As soon as we got home from school, we'd eat a snack, change our clothes and hurry to carry in wood. Unless we had the wood in, we couldn't listen to our favorite radio program, *The Lone Ranger*.

After that, the girls either helped with supper or milked the cows, while the boys slopped the hogs, fed the horses and gave hay to the cows. We also milked those cows before we went to school in the morning; I can still feel the biting cold of early winter mornings.

The chore I disliked the most was harvesting sweet potatoes. The first day of school I ever missed in second grade was because of those sweet potatoes. In fact, we all had to skip school and help; it had turned cold early and we were running a race against the weather.

My hands were *so* cold as I graveled those potatoes. I hated it, but didn't complain. We knew it would mean money for shoes and oth-

The Nelson sisters, Marjean Viksna (left) and Eleanor McClure, dressed up for shocking grain in the 1930's near Woonsocket, South Dakota.

er items, so we helped all we could. Even at that age, we knew how to be responsible.   —*Ruby Neese Liberty, North Carolina*

My younger sister and I had to chop cotton in the summers. We'd get up early and put on old shorts, shirts and beat-up tennis shoes, then fill our water jugs.

When we were younger, we hoed just in the cotton patches. But as we got older, we also hoed in the fields, which had much longer rows.

On one especially long hot day, the rows seemed *so* long that I wasn't sure whether I could make it to the end, then come back down another long row to reach the water jug.

But somehow I *did* make it. And on that day, I learned if I could make it down those long cotton rows, I could make it through anything else in life.

I've since remembered that, especially during difficult times in my life. So far, I've been able to endure trying times and have always emerged a little stronger.   —*Lynn Buchanan Mountainburg, Arkansas*

We all dreaded gathering eggs when darkness had settled in, knowing we'd get pecked by our Rhode Island Reds if they were in a bad mood, or find a snake curled up in an empty nest.

So my brother Don and I developed a technique to help us out. We used a corncob to "feel" the empty nest, or to wedge up against the side of a hen's head so it couldn't peck us as we gathered eggs. Small wonder that we were glad when the job of egg gathering was passed on to younger siblings!

But we weren't the only ones with a creative egg-gathering technique. My baby brother, Bud, also developed a great way of collecting eggs when the job was passed on to him.

We found out about it when a neighbor stopped by to chat with Mom while Bud—who was about 10 years old at the time—was on his way to gather eggs. Our neighbor warned him, "Watch those hens, Bud—they'll peck you." Bud assured her that this would not happen because he wore a glove.

She said, "But those old hens will peck right through the glove." Bud replied, "Not through *this* glove!"

See, Bud would plop a *catcher's mitt* over a poor chicken's head, then reach around with his other hand to pluck the eggs out from under her. I rolled on the floor with laughter, and Mom laughed, too, and shook her head.

Our neighbor, being neither an athlete nor an egg gatherer, only looked quizzical. We realized that only a child who did daily battle with the Rhode Island Reds could understand and appreciate Bud's approach!
                    —*Betty McVaigh, Carrollton, Georgia*

For a little girl, life on a farm that was 13 miles of dirt, rock and chuckholes from the nearest town was not one of carefree play all day.

Even at the tender age of 5, I contributed to the daily routine of farm life, always willing to do whatever Papa or Mama said needed to be done, and I wasn't really fearful of anything.

Because our family ate a lot of corn bread, we always had a need for corn-meal. But keeping enough on hand during the summer was very difficult because of all the other chores we had to do.

One time, when I was a little older, we had used up all of our meal and needed more badly. So Papa got a 5-gallon lard can, removed the bottom and opened the can down the seam. With the inside of the can facing up, he nailed it to the cellar door, gave me a hammer and a No. 8 nail, and told me to make nail holes all over the center portion of the tin.

When I'd made enough holes to please Papa, he took the can loose from the door of the cellar, gently bowed the can into a semicircle and tacked it to a board in that position. The outward portion of the nail holes served as a grate. He then got a large bucket of dried corn on the cob and put me to grating it.

I had to rub the ears of corn up and down the grate, catching the bolted meal in a large pan. I had to be careful so as not to cut my hands on the punctured tin. When I had grated the pan full of meal, Mama would prepare our corn bread for dinner. In spite of the hard work for such a little girl, the bread was so good and tasty with fresh cow milk over it!

I remember grating a lot of corn that summer. I also recall my two brothers, two sisters and I being ill with a fever almost every other day. By the end of that summer, Mama counted that we had taken 49

Even the littlest hands could help out with chores on the farm.

50-cent bottles of Grove's Tasteless Chill Tonic!

Whether or not all of that chill tonic, along with an occasional hefty dose of Black Draught, kept us from getting worse or made us better, I don't know. But the vivid memory of my grating corn is forever coupled with that "chill tonic summer".

—*Earlene Edwards, Santa Maria, California*

As a child, I learned to work hard, beginning at a very young age.

My list of chores included gathering eggs, peeling potatoes, filling kerosene lamps, cleaning the lamp chimneys, helping saw, split and carry wood for winter warmth and cooking, and carrying water—this before I was even able to carry a full bucket.

My brothers and I would help sow, weed and harvest the vegetable garden, particularly planting and digging potatoes and picking and shelling peas.

And since I was the oldest, I often had to care for the younger children while Mom and Dad butchered, milked their dairy herd or put up hay. Washing dishes was usually my job, too; I started that when I was small enough to still need a stool to reach the dishpan!

Perhaps the chore I liked the least was washing the syrup buckets the milk was kept in for our use. These buckets, with tight-fitting lids, could be hung in the creek so the milk would stay cool and not

Bringing the cows in from the pasture for evening milking was an enjoyable chore for many kids.

sour. I had to wash thoroughly under the rims of these buckets, and there was a sharp edge that could cut your fingers.

The fun job was getting the milk cows from a far pasture for evening milking during the summer. It was more than a mile each way, but we loved walking the distance.

Hard work at home prepared us well for the future—and left us little time to get into any serious trouble! —*Roberta Nadler, Augusta, Missouri*

My great-grandparents were in their 60's when they took me in to raise me on their farm in Indiana.

Grandpa had about a 2-acre vegetable and berry patch and a 2-acre orchard. He sold his produce to a local grocery store in town, so it was important to get up early and pick "morning-fresh" produce.

I didn't mind helping with chores, except for picking strawberries. You see, the strawberries would ripen just about the time school was out for the summer—and I thought I'd get an extra half hour of sleep.

But every other morning, Grandma would stand at the bottom of the stairs and holler, "Peggy, it's time to get up—you have to help 'Dad' pick strawberries."

I'd lay there for a few minutes, hoping that she wouldn't call again, but a short time later, I'd hear her yell, "Peggy, you'd better get out of that bed now because Dad just took the boxes and went to the strawberry patch."

Well, when I'd hear that, I'd hit the floor before

J.C. Allen and Son

she was finished and start throwing on clothes while mumbling to myself about how I hated to pick strawberries.

You might be surprised to learn that I have a small strawberry patch of my own now. I love to eat them, but I still hate to pick them!

—*Peggy Smith McIlwain, Iron City, Georgia*

I'll always remember how hard my dad and I worked in the 1920's and 1930's to get a year's supply of firewood to fuel the kitchen range and the heater.

We'd go to the woods with axes and a crosscut hand saw. The saw had a blade about 4 feet long with a handle on each end. After notching the tree with the ax, we'd use the saw on the opposite side to complete the cut. It was backbreaking work.

All that hard work sawing logs sure paid off come the middle of winter.

J.C. Allen and Son

The fallen tree then had to be "brushed out" by cutting the branches from the log. With the team of horses and a sledge or a wagon, we'd haul the logs home and unload them near the house.

When we felt that we had enough for the follow-ing winter supply, we would arrange for a crew of neighbors to help saw the logs into stove-size blocks. Dad had a large 8-horsepower gasoline engine and a large circular saw rig. The logs were placed on a hinged table and pushed into the whirling saw blade. The cut blocks were caught and tossed away from the machine by one of the crew.

At the end of this job, we'd have mountains of cut wood. Then came another huge task—splitting and piling the wood. We used axes, a maul and wedges for splitting. We'd stack the split logs in a woodshed, where we'd let it dry for a year.

Each day we had to haul in a day's supply of wood—not to mention the ashes that had to be carried out daily. So you can see that there was a lot of hard labor in making wood to heat our house and provide cooking fuel.

—*Arthur Laehn*
Clintonville, Wisconsin

When Grandma gathered eggs, I enjoyed going along to help. We'd go into the henhouse, where the hens would be in their little cubbyhole nests, softly crooning a sing-song clucking.

You could tell when a hen had laid an egg. She'd proudly and loudly announce it to the world with some distinctive clucking. To a hen, it must have been a thing of pride each time it happened.

The hens were never pleased to see me. They liked Grandma coming into their house, but I made them a little nervous. Grandma would carefully slip her hand under each hens' warm little body and bring out one, two or even three eggs. Each hen would lay only one, but often another hen would lay her egg

Egg gathering could be a rewarding job—if you didn't get your hand pecked!

in the same nest. Grandma taught me how to reach under the hens. But they resented a child doing this rather private thing, and would often peck at me with their little dagger-like beaks. That could really hurt!

Most of the time, I'd just watch Grandma fill her egg basket. She'd let me help her put the clean eggs into cardboard cases to be sold in town at the end of the week. —*Pat Leek, Laporte, Minnesota*

Everyone in our family of seven had their own chores to do on our small farm in northern Indiana.

When I was 8 years old, my chore was taking care of the chickens. This included gathering and cleaning the eggs, feeding and giving water to the chickens.

The worst part was cleaning the eggs, but I made the best of it by turning a few of those chickens into my pets. "Henry" the rooster and "Dusty", "Henrietta" and "Smoky" were among my favorites.

I fed them oyster shells out of my hand and talked to them every morning and evening during chores. I imagined that they understood every word I said and were answering me with a cluck or a scratch.

I spent countless hours trying to talk them into doing tricks, like sitting or standing in a row, but to no avail. My mother said she would look out the kitchen window and see the chickens following me around the barnyard. I guess deep down they wanted to understand me, but all that talking

was too much for a chicken brain to comprehend.

Now I'm 1,000 miles away from that farm. I cherish those memories and others, and am thankful that I grew up on a farm. —*Twylla Eversole Bell*
Irving, Texas

Taking care of animals was my favorite chore when I was growing up on the farm. We raised sheep, hogs, chickens and cows, and, of course, I had lots of cats, too.

We always let the sheep into a pen at night. During lambing time, I'd follow Dad to the barn to check on them. Sometimes we got twins or triplets. Once in a while, I'd get a chance to feed some on a bottle and make pets of them.

When I was very little, I saw Dad putting rubber bands on the lamb's tails. I did the same thing to one of my cats. Good thing Dad found the cat in time, or she'd have been without a tail!

The little calves were always very tame. I would pet, curry, wash—even ride them. They were easy to load in a truck to sell or, if Dad kept them for cows, he would have the most gentle cows around.

I never cared much for chickens, though. One time I was in the chicken pen and a rooster jumped on me. From that time on, I'd throw a little corn over the fence and then while they were fighting over it, I'd put feed in the feeder.

I always took care of the cats. One year an old tom cat killed the baby kittens every time some were born, so I put them in a bushel basket with a lid. The mother cat would meow when she wanted in or out of the basket. When they were a little older, I would put them in only at night. They all lived.

I was a lot younger than my brother and sister, so I had to entertain myself. Guess I was a real tom "boy".
—*Marjorie Traxler, Exline, Iowa*

In the winter of 1936, my husband-to-be cut wood to sell and to use after we got married in 1937.

My father helped and also cut wood to earn money for himself. Together, my husband and father cut over 800 racks of wood, which sold for $1.86 for a rack and a half.

My husband took a tractor with a buzz saw on it and earned $1.25 an hour sawing wood for other people. How many young people would work for that nowadays?
—*Winifred Lane*
Corsicana, Texas

Being a typical child, I was never fond of chores—but that didn't stop me from having to do my share!

The job I hated most was pumping water for the livestock. In one small pasture, we had a well and a large stock tank. My oldest brother and I were responsible for keeping that tank filled.

We'd pump it full, then let the cattle in and pump like crazy all the time they were drinking, trying to keep it full. No matter how hard we pumped, they'd almost empty it before they got their fill.

The one chore I *did* enjoy was gathering eggs. My parents kept lots of laying hens, as the eggs and cream paid for our weekly staples plus whatev-

er feed was needed from time to time for the chickens and livestock.

The summer I was either 10 or 11, we were gathering around 100 eggs a day. Mother told me more than once to always gather the eggs from the barn first, but one day I decided to do it my way and gather from the henhouse first.

Thirsty horses always appreciated a cool drink of freshly pumped water.

By the time I reached the barn, I had almost a full bucket of eggs. While gathering in the barn, I stepped on a pitchfork that had been thrown down in the hay, tines up. I was barefoot, and one of the tines went completely through my foot at the base of my toes. Of course, I spilled the bucket and broke most of the eggs.

I wasn't taken to a doctor. My folks kept me off my foot for a few days and doctored it with kerosene and turpentine. Needless to say, my brother and I both received a stern lecture—me for not following orders and him for leaving a pitchfork laying in the hay.
—*Juanita Elbrader*
Mountain Home, Arkansas

Our family ranch is situated in the southeastern corn belt of Oregon in what is called "high desert".

My brother and I were expected to do a wide variety of chores on the ranch, which included feeding chickens, pigs, orphan lambs and calves; milking cows; weeding the garden; and saddling and taking care of the horses that we rode 3 miles to school each day. There was only one chore that neither of us ever really learned to relish, and that was picking the four to six long rows of raspberries each summer!

Our mother would call us out of our warm beds at 5 a.m., reminding us that we must get the picking done before the hot sun hit the patch. We often got distracted playing games or tossing dirt clods at each other.

When Mother heard any ruckus, we'd soon be called back to our task. For our labors, we were awarded the grand sum of 10¢ per row.

I used to think I'd never, ever want to eat or see another raspberry, but now that I'm retired and living in the town of Burns some 50 miles from the ranch, I've cultivated a small garden plot in the backyard.

And believe it or not, there's a short row of raspberry bushes included, which provides me with freezer jam and fresh fruit, plus some to share with friends and relatives.
—*Shirley Thompson*
Burns, Oregon

We had a large family, and while we had a lot of fun together, we also had to work hard. When I was only 10, I had to help my brother check our barbed wire fences. I'd carry the staple bucket and he'd replace the staples where needed.

When my sister and I were about 12 years old, we'd have to take hoes and cut weeds out of the corn rows while Dad cultivated our river bottomland.

We'd wear big straw hats for this kind of work. We would put big leaves from some kind of willow

tree under the hats to keep our heads cooler. At the end of a row, there'd be a brown jug of water wrapped in a wet gunnysack to keep it cool. I remember well how good that water tasted when we were so tired, hot and thirsty.

When we were through, sometimes Dad would lift each of us up on a horse for the ride home.
—*Cora Sechrest, Chenoa, Illinois*

Romus Hight (left) and his brother, Ray, stopped weeding just long enough to have their picture taken.

One of my least favorite chores on our Indiana farm when I was about 10 years old was hoeing in the cornfield.

We each had our own hoe and the field was kept clean of most weeds. There were exceptions, however. If my brother and I were hoeing in rows next to each other and a weed was exactly in the center row, neither of us would hoe it out.

We became very good at judging distances with the naked eye. It became a game with us, and if it was too close to call, we would sometimes measure the distance with a hoe handle.

This game made the task less tedious. You can understand why Dad sometimes put us on either side of him in the field as we hoed!

One of the great hazards of hoeing corn was the propensity to cut off cornstalks. We never wanted to bend over to pull a weed, so we hoed as close to the stalk as possible.

Sometimes it was too close, and we'd cut the stalk off with the weed. Dad kept our hoes very sharp, but to him, that was no excuse for that kind of mischief. So if we cut off a stalk of corn, it always got a quick and decent burial. We didn't want any incriminating evidence lying around.

We look back on those days very fondly. But during the drought years of the 1930's, those hot, dry 100-degree days were a thing to be reckoned with, and added to our storehouse of memories.

—Dorothy Doerflein Levermann
Highland Heights, Kentucky

By the time I was 11, I had a regular schedule of work to do each morning. I'd arrive in the barn at 5 a.m. and chase down 25 milk cows, scrape down their droppings and fluff up the straw under each cow. I'd clean out their mangers and feed each one their grain, soybeans, oil-meal and salt.

Next I'd get the cans, pails and wash water ready, clean the cows' udders and milk all 25 cows. Then I'd put the milk into 10-gallon cans and store them in a water tank, or later, in an electric cooler, to keep them cold. Following that, I'd wash all the pails, strainers and other milking equipment.

I'd feed each of my 15 to 20 calves with a pail; go up in the 40-foot-high silo and toss down silage for the cows, then feed them; go up in the hayloft and toss down about 20 to 30 pounds of hay for the cows and calves; and toss down corn for our eight horses.

When feeding was finished, I had to harness two horses, hitch them to a manure spreader and clean the barn. This meant using a fork or shovel to put all the cow manure, bedding and old hay onto the spreader. The horses would pull the spreader out in the field, where either the spreader would distribute it or I'd do it by hand.

I'd return to the barn, unhitch and unharness the horses, load the milk cans on a sled or wagon and take them to the creamery—1-1/2 miles away.

Upon returning home, I'd wash up, change my clothes, eat breakfast and get ready for school. I rode my bike the 1-1/2 miles to school, which started at 8 a.m. But when I went to high school, I had to have all of this work done in time to catch the bus at 7:05 a.m. This was my routine, every Monday through Friday.

On Saturdays and Sundays, we had a full day of work, ranging from grinding feed to sawing and hauling wood for our wood-burning stove—we used wood to heat the house and cook the food.

This was a lot of work for such a young man. No wonder I'm still tired when I go to visit my grandchildren!

—Curtis Nelson, *Eagan, Minnesota*

Come January, after the holidays had passed, Mom would set up two round washtubs on the long bench in the basement and prepare to strip feathers. She'd fill one of the tubs with feathers and down from the geese and ducks butchered in fall.

Then, in her spare time, she'd strip the quills from

Gathering eggs meant watching out for snakes—and that mean ol' rooster, too!

Plucking feathers was hard work, but it was worth it to feel that down pillow under your head every night.

the feathers, throwing the quills in the empty tub. When we got old enough, we'd help her, wearing dust caps to cover our hair. We'd spend all our spare time stripping those feathers.

We usually spent a few hours a day doing this until the job was finished. It was a fun time for storytelling, mother-and-daughter talk and companionship. And all the while, the tub would gradually fill with clean, fresh-stripped feathers.

Then Mom would buy pillow ticking by the yard, stitch it into pillowcases and fill each one with 2.5 to 3 pounds of feathers. Sometimes there was enough for 3 pairs of pillows. That was a lot of feathers—no sneezing on the job!

—*Marianna Ostrowski*
New Boston, Michigan

My family worked as sharecroppers on a farm in western Kentucky during the Great Depression. Farming without modern conveniences was hard, sweaty work, and Papa and my brothers spent long hours in the fields.

Watermelons were our cash crop. After Papa worked up the ground, it was my job—along with the landlord's son—to plant the seeds, which we poked into the ground with a stick or our fingers.

When the melons were ripe enough to sell, Papa and my brother would take a wagonload to the county seat, 5 miles away. They'd leave early in the morning and come home at night. Then Papa would cut the stems of the melons he wanted to sell the next day.

It was our job to carry these melons to the shed the next day before Papa got home. One day, my older sisters and the landlord's daughter refused to carry any melons in. That left me and the landlord's son. I was only 11 or 12, and he was even younger, but we got busy carrying those melons.

The day was hot and it was hard work, so we decided to use a wheelbarrow. That was a lot easier and faster, and all went well until somehow the wheelbarrow overturned, bursting two huge melons! Now, we both loved watermelon. We were allowed to eat the smaller ones, but were supposed to save bigger ones to sell.

But under the circumstances, we quickly decided what to do—we dove right in, dirty hands and all, starting with the juicy hearts. We ate until we were stuffed. Then we gathered up the remains and took them to the hog pen, where every last bit of evidence was devoured.

I waited several months to tell Papa about our little accident. He hadn't even missed the two melons and laughed when I told him how we got rid of the "evidence".

—*Faye Edmunds*
Hopkinsville, Kentucky

I'll never figure out how our mother got us out in the woods every year to pick those little green, sour, obnoxious gooseberries. But every year, there we were, out in the timber among the poison ivy, snakes, mosquitoes, gnats and prickly underbrush, buckets hanging from our arms and determined looks glued to our faces.

We'd pick gooseberries every May until there weren't any left; in those days, we never let anything go to waste. Actually, they were kind of good—as long as they were saturated with sugar, poured over hot biscuits and smothered with thick cream!

If she could, Mom would accompany us, saying how much she enjoyed being outdoors and away from the old cookstove. She couldn't stay away for long, not with that all-important noon meal for a hungry family of nine. So my two younger sisters and I would toil away for hours just to get a gallon bucket filled before noon. This wasn't entirely impossible—if we were lucky enough to find an unpicked patch.

Could we then wash them and eat them as we did with strawberries? No sirree! They each had to be stemmed, one by one. To do this, you had to pluck two sides of each berry with a fingernail. Such painstaking, tedious work was actually worse than the picking to active children like us. But sometimes one of our grandmothers would come over and help us with the berry stemming. They'd set on the front porch and visit while they worked and didn't seem to mind at all.

Believe it or not, there were people in town who would actually *buy* gooseberries. They would pay us 25¢ a gallon, which was a lot of money to a country kid in those days. This provided great incentive to pick berries until we were ready to drop. One older lady must have liked them very much—she'd always call and order a gallon or two.

As I got older, I rebelled and opted to stay in the house and iron clothes or fix dinner—anything but pick gooseberries!

—*Auda Bratcher*
Raytown, Missouri

To this day, I prefer outside work. That's probably because I was Daddy's helper, since he didn't have any boys. I helped him with milking and feeding cows and horses. I could put the gear on a horse as good as he could—well, almost.

Once Daddy was gone and Mama and my sisters were canning tomatoes. I offered to hitch up the team and haul them to the house on a sled. Then something went wrong—I think I crossed the lines. Anyway, the horses got scared and ran off, scattering tomatoes everywhere. I didn't try that again for a long time!

Another chore I'll never forget is making lye soap. Every year we set aside a day to make soap in a big black kettle. All we used was water, grease and pure lye. We'd cook it so many hours, then take it off the fire and let it "set up".

The next morning, we'd cut it into 4-inch by 4-inch blocks and lay them on a plank to dry. The soap was light brown in color, but did a great job on laundry. We also used it to wash dishes—we even used it to wash our hair. It did a good job.   —*Helen Kennedy*
Owensboro, Kentucky

Like author in accompanying story, this young woman enjoyed outdoor work more than indoor chores.

Bringing the cows home near East Albany,
Vermont; inset, loading hay into the loft.

Clockwise from top left: farmer prepares to milk "Ol' Bossy"; winter fun gathering eggs in Iowa; farmer feeding cattle in Twin Falls, Idaho; wintertime hog feeding on Midwest farm; homeward bound; brushing up a barn in Iowa.

Hens turned in a good day's work for this farm wife (right). This page, continuing clockwise: selling hay to a neighbor in Port Huron, Michigan; wheelbarrow at rest; another wheelbarrow being put through its paces—carefully; unloading golden grain in Iowa. Opposite page: Farmer prepares to call it a day (to do some sight-seeing perhaps?); inset, pitching hay during threshing season.

Bonnie Nance

Julie Habel

Julie Habel

Tom Narwid

74

Opposite page, clockwise from top left: little girl gets some horse sense from Dad; fieldwork is never done; farmer tending to bulls near West Fairlee, Vermont; harvesting grain is a family affair on this Iowa farm.

Cows get hay from on high in above photo. Continuing clockwise: it's follow the leader during feeding time; farmer prepares to feed hogs during Iowa winter; Belgian horsepower helps Kentucky farmer.

4

J.C. Allen and Son

Each autumn, I think back to a very special event that occurred when I was in fourth grade. My teacher had given our class an assignment to collect various types of leaves and put them in a scrapbook, along with information about the trees from which they came.

Now, fall is a busy time for farmers. Nonetheless, one lovely Sunday afternoon, my father made time to tromp with me through the woods behind our barn and collect leaves. I can still remember the sunshine streaming through the trees, which were colored lovely reds, oranges and golds. And I still remember how he told me about the leaves and some of the trees, which were much smaller when he was my age.

I don't recall what grade I received for my leaf project. But I do know that my walk through the woods that fall day allowed me to have a wonderful time with my father on our family farm.

—*Karl Wood Winkler, Fairfax, Virginia*

For a change of pace on our wheat farm in western Oklahoma, my dad would occasionally try his hand at growing cotton. I distinctly remember one chilly early morning being excited about helping him plant cotton with a wheat drill.

Dad only planted a few acres, so he would purchase just enough seed for what he needed. Since cotton has to be planted in rows farther apart than wheat, Dad plugged every other hole on the drill.

My job was to ride the back of the drill, lean into the drill box and push the limited cottonseed into the open holes as we bumped around the field. On this particular morning, the air was just a little bit too nippy for me.

Dad soon realized my dilemma, so after the last bag of seed was dumped into the drill box, he tore a head-sized hole in the closed end of the bag and slipped it over my head and arms. The heavyweight paper bag served as a wonderful insulator from the frosty air. —*Rhonda Kliewer, Clovis, California*

Harvesting corn was one of the things I liked best about farming in the 1920's, from planting time to silo-filling time.

We'd put a special deep box on the wagon. Inside, we'd put in what looked like a barn door on edge. Then, as the horses pulled the wagon through the corn, we'd "snap out" the ears of corn from the stalks and toss them in the wagon. When they hit that vertical board, they made a "bang", then fell into the wagon box; that's why it was called a "bang board".

After the corn was put in the

Wagon with "bang board"—named for the sound created when it was hit with ears of picked corn.

barn, the neighbors gathered for a husking bee. Each person used a special tool called a husking peg; most of them were made of hardwood, and later some were metal.

Both are now antiques, and corn is harvested by a mechanical picker. The old time corncrib is long gone, except in Amish Country. —*Walt Thayer*
Wenatchee, Washington

We were used to rough winters while I was growing up in upstate New York, near Lake Ontario. But a storm we had in the winter of 1946 was unique—it didn't stop snowing for 2 weeks!

I was 8 years old at the time, and my brother was 5. We lived on a dairy farm and had 100 head of cattle as well as many other kinds of animals to care for.

The snow fell until it was up to 10 feet deep in most places, and the roads were impassable for anything, including the snowplows. My brother and I played on top of snowdrifts that were level with the power lines. We were stranded!

Our first problem was getting from the house to the barn to feed and milk the cows. There was no other choice but to dig a tunnel, and oh, what a job that was.

Our next problem was the milk, which we were unable to take to the local milk factory. Our wonderful mother, trying to salvage all she could, came up with an idea. She scrubbed and disinfected our wringer washer, separated the cream from the milk, poured the pure cream in the washer and turned it on. Ta da—butter! Mom put it up in crocks and sold it after the roads were cleared.

It took huge rotary snowblowers to finally dig us out. It was a winter I'll never forget.
—*Merry VanBuren, Roanoke, Virginia*

Some 80 years ago, my father carved an 80-acre farm out of sagebrush 2 miles west of Eden, Idaho. I was born on this farm and spent the first 7 years of my life there.

I especially loved the summers, when you could see the wheat, corn and alfalfa growing, as well as our orchard of fruit trees and the family garden. The high point was the threshing-bee season, with the steam engine and grain separator, and the neighboring farmers with their horses and wagons.

However, I didn't like the shrill steam whistle, which the engine man pulled on early mornings, noon and evenings. I would cover my ears with my hands. At one noon meal, I remember watching two older gray-haired men scoop up green peas with their knives and roll them into their mouths. This really amazed me to no end. I've never again seen a performance like that one. —*Robert Gunning*
Sacramento, California

There was a huge chestnut tree on my father's 200-acre farm in West Virginia, where we lived 'til I was 6. It stood up the lane from our house and yielded bushels of chestnuts each fall.

I remember when I was 5 and begged to accompany my sisters one bright fall Saturday morning as they collected chestnuts. This would have been after

On the back of this picture, sent in by Chuck Halla of Hartford, Wisconsin, are printed the words, "Snow, snow, snow". That says it all!

the first deep frost, which caused the burrs to open.

I was allowed to go and, needless to say, I returned with plenty of prickly burrs in my fingers. But I was happy to learn about gathering chestnuts—and roasting them in the hot coals of the fire that night!

As for winters, I remember my father's sleigh bells, which he sometimes put on the horses' harnesses when he took us for rides. I recall one particularly deep snowfall when he harnessed the team and took us for a sleigh ride into town, snuggled under a huge bearskin. The horses enjoyed the outing after spending many long winter days in the barn.

One horse named "George"—part Percheron, part Arabian—was always a challenge to my father. He was very strong and enjoyed being taken out to pull the sleigh. George loved the sleigh bells and would arch his neck, raise his tail and prance sideways, lifting his feet like a gaited animal, attracting much attention from passersby.
—*Mary Clay*
Palm Coast, Florida

During the Depression, farmers around the small German community of Fredericksburg, Texas helped each other with the yearly threshing. In those years, not many farmers had a threshing machine. So all the farmers who wanted their wheat or oats harvested would join together in a "band".

On threshing day, my mother and the other ladies would be doing chores by 4 a.m. After that, they'd cook a hearty breakfast—usually bacon, eggs and homemade bread. After eating, the men would begin working while the women would start baking pies and cleaning the kitchen.

Farm families eagerly waited for the threshing crew to arrive at their farm.

Around 9:30 or 10 a.m., the women packed "lunch", which was actually a snack that consisted of the just-baked pies, cakes baked a day or two before, sandwiches and coffee. The women would ride to the field on a wagon to serve the food.

The women returned to the house on the next wagon to begin the huge task of cooking "dinner", or the noon meal, which would include meat prepared over an open fire, sweet rice, potatoes, prunes, dried apples, green beans and other vegetables.

After that meal, the women washed dishes and prepared another lunch, which was the same as the morning snack. After that, they'd make "supper", which was usually the same as dinner. It was a never-ending cycle of meal preparation. And it continued at each farm in the band until the harvest was completed.
—*Alma Eckert Pehl*
Fredericksburg, Texas

On our diversified farm in the Arkansas Ozarks, my dad always had one field of sugarcane that kept us busy during harvest. We'd start by stripping the leaves by hand from the stalks—they made for good cow fodder (nothing went to waste).

After that, one of my older brothers would cut the stalks with a scythe, then chop off the heads. Some heads were saved for seed and the rest were fed to the chickens. I loved to cut off a joint of the cane, peel it and chew it to get the sweet juice. It was a real treat.

The stalks then were taken to the local gristmill. There they'd hitch a long pole that was connected to the mill. It was my job to drive the horse in a circle to activate it. The stalks were fed through rollers that squeezed out the juice. Refuse cane stalks were known as mash—also good for cow fodder.

After that, Dad made molasses. First, he'd boil the juice on a huge furnace. As it boiled, a green scum would form on top, which we'd skim off with long-handled scoops and dump into a large container—good food for the hogs.

When the juice had cooked to a thick syrup and turned a golden color, we'd empty it into 5-gallon wooden kegs. When we finished with our molasses, we did the same for one neighbor after another until the whole community had their cane crop processed. Dad retained a certain portion of the molasses as a toll.

This golden supply provided a delicious breakfast treat on biscuits. Occasionally, my mother would cook the syrup after supper in an iron kettle. When the syrup candied, she'd empty it into butter platters until it was cool enough to pull. Everyone took a portion and began pulling until it was stiff enough to break into pieces.

J.C. Allen and Son

Endless fields of grain meant plenty of work come harvesttime.

At the time, it was the custom in rural communities for the teacher of the one-room school to spend a night with each family. When the teacher came to our house, we'd "pull candy" after supper.
—*Erma Humphreys, Dodge City, Kansas*

During the summer of 1941, I was 18 years old and desperately needed money to pay for my junior college tuition in fall. Working on a local threshing crew was my only hope.

The pay was good—$3 a day, as I recall. And you were also fed and given a place to sleep, even if it was just a mattress on the floor of a spare room in the farmer's house.

There were two threshing operations in the area where I lived in southern Minnesota, and coincidentally, they were owned by brothers-in-law. I had worked for one of them the previous season, but he wasn't hiring that year. My father knew both of the men and tried to help me get a job with the other rig. He explained that I needed the work because I was saving money to go back to college in the fall.

The owner's reaction was negative—he said he "didn't want no college boy". My dad explained that, while I was trying to go to college, I had grown up on the family farm and could harness and drive horses, load grain, milk cows, slop pigs, clean manure from barns and anything else that needed to be done. He also added that I had worked the previous season for his brother in law.

Now, it was common knowledge in the neighborhood that for some reason, there was no love lost between the two brothers-in-law. At this point, my prospective employer looked at me again and said, "Well, anybody who can work for that so-and-so can work for me. You're hired." All the other hired hands were men 30 years old or older.

It was tough work. Because it was critical to thresh the crop as quickly as possible after it was cut and shocked, the threshing machine often started as early as 5 a.m. and didn't shut down until dark or until that particular farmer's fields were finished. At times, lights were turned on at the rig so we could finish the last few loads.

At the end of the threshing season, I felt sure my employer was satisfied with my work. He proved it by offering me—the 18-year-old "college boy"—a permanent job on his farm. I thanked him, but explained again that my goal had been to earn money for college, and that was what I must do.

But I've always been grateful to this former employer, not only for the financial assistance the job gave me, but for the satisfaction he expressed at the end of the season with his offer of permanent employment.   —*Frank Durfey, Sequim, Washington*

I can vividly recall hog-killing time in Sumerduck, the small rural village in Virginia where I grew up. The season started in mid-November and went through mid-December, but preparation began several weeks prior as we'd split dry kindling wood, purchase spices and cornmeal for seasoning, dig a pit for the scalding tub, and get the equipment and utensils scheduled.

Like threshing, hog killing was a community project. One farmer owned the scalding tub, another had a sausage grinder and still another had the big cast-iron black pots. Scheduling hog killing was built around who was using the utensils/equipment on which day. I looked forward to riding with my dad to go to the farms to acquire the utensils and arrange for the men to help.

Butchering day started early. The fire had to be built and the water boiling in the scalding tub by 7:30 a.m. The butchering took until around 4:30 p.m. Everyone kept busy, for there was much to do—the slaughtering, cutting and trimming the meat, keeping the fires stoked and the knives sharp, stirring the big pots of liver pudding and scrapple over open fires and grinding the sausage. We did take time, though, to eat the large dinner my mom would prepare for the hungry men.

My job was to help "put the meat down" for curing by covering it with a mixture of salt, meal and borax. Then I helped knead and roll the sausage

Until the invention of modern combines, threshing was usually a community affair.

into 1-pound rolls. We always had a No. 2 washtub full of sausage.

My parents would sell some of the fresh sausage and meat and the old hams left from the previous year. Proceeds from this paid the bills and bought our Christmas gifts. I recall when a hog died in the fall it meant fewer Christmas presents that year.

The community project of hog killing is now long gone in my home village. But for many families, it's a memory of the "good ol' days" that will be passed on for generations to come.   —*Marlene Peyton*
Fredericksburg, Virginia

Big snowstorms were common when I was growing up on the farm. Strong winds would create high snowdrifts and near-zero visibility, while temperatures would drop by the hour.

During these storms, we carried pails of water to the cattle. I can still see them dipping their heads into those pails and almost emptying them in one big slurp.

We'd also carry straw in from the big stack in back of the barn and bed the cows and horses down belly-deep for the long night. The cows would watch us fork the fresh, new straw high between them. In the calf barn, the little calves would look so cute in the deep straw, especially when just their heads and ears stuck up.

At night, "Fanny", our collie, always slept on the pile of hay in front of the cows. The cats would curl up and go to sleep in the straw between cows that were lying close together.

The deep snow provided us with lots of fun. We had a lot of rail fences, so our long lane and barnyard became a fantasyland, with 4- and 5-foot drifts in every shape imaginable. We'd run up and over and down them, squealing with laughter. Covered with snow, we looked like little running snowmen.

On the hill by our pigpen, we'd break a sled trail. Where the drifts were deep, our older brothers would shovel the snow out. Then we'd run, one behind the other, and jump onto our sleds on our bellies and follow the trail down the hill. After the trail was really packed down, we could go all the way down to the corner post—about 1/8 of a mile!

We did most of our sledding at night. With so much white snow and a nice moon, why, our hill was ever so bright, like God had a special light on just for us. In the wide-open space, we'd pick out the Big Dipper, the North Star, Venus and Mars.

Many nights, we'd stand on the hill and watch the northern lights, standing in wonder as those fingers of pastel pinks, blues and light greens streaked and flashed in the sky. Soon we'd run to the house and tell Mother and Dad—it was too great not to share.   —*Robert Witkovsky, Bay City, Michigan*

A fresh meal makes braving a winter snowstorm a little easier for these critters.

Threshing time meant busy days on our farm. My Great-Uncle Lou owned the local threshing machine, and I can still see him come banging and clanging up the country road very early in the morning.

Uncle Lou sat so straight on that big machine, with a sparkling-clean, long-sleeved blue chambray shirt and a pair of overalls just as fresh. He also wore a wide-brimmed straw hat.

Sometimes he would come up to the house and sit under the shade tree for a rest. I was glad for a chance to leave the busy kitchen, as I was the "gopher" for water, corncobs, wood or whatever was needed at the moment. I'd take him a glass of cold lemonade and visit for a spell.

I wish I could recall the stories that he told me, but all I remember is a little ditty he would recite: "Here we sit in the shade, drinking lemonade and stirring it with a rusty spade."

There was a lot of cooking and baking to be done. One year, my mom hurriedly got a jar of cherries from the shelf in the cellar, and made a pie. When the men began eating dessert, she remembered that she had canned a few jars of unpitted cherries, and, in her haste, had grabbed one of those. She never lived that one down, but with her great sense of humor, she tried to make them believe that it was a trick she had played on them.

—*Darlene Smith, Rockford, Illinois*

My favorite memory from growing up in rural Kentucky was hog-killing time in the fall. My dad and several of our neighbors would always help each other out on those busy days.

I can still remember the crisp November mornings and the steam rising from the big open kettle where the lard was rendered.

Usually by late evening, it would be time to grind the meat into sausage. We would all take turns at the grinder, a machine attached to a large board. We placed the board on two chairs and had two people sit on it for anchors. Then came the grinding. The grinder would squeeze fresh meat into a large pan below.

My mother would mix all the delectable ingredients into the meat and we would get ready to make "patties" for freezing. Then came the best part. She'd fry several patties to see if she had used just the right amount of sage.

By this time, it would be getting dark, and the smell of that sausage frying and homemade biscuits baking was irresistible. I don't know if we were just hungry from the hard work or what, but those biscuits and sausage were the best eating of the year.

We would have plenty of good sausage and meat in our freezer to do us until the next year, and I couldn't wait until it was hog-killing time again!

—*Monica Barrett, Booneville, Kentucky*

I remember the cold winter nights on our farm, when the cows were bedded down for the night, the chickens were shut in and all the other farm animals—horses, goats and sheep—had been tended to.

We didn't have any television back then. Instead, we would all gather around the old wood-burning cookstove with the door

Feathers seem to keep these chickens warm enough to "talk".

open and eat popcorn while listening to the Wheeling, West Virginia radio station, or listen to Mother and Father tell stories. It was a very peaceful and delightful time for us. —*Linda Kirkey, Dexter, New York*

The arrival of fall on our farm near Dysart, Iowa meant it was time to pick corn. That required being in the field by daylight, and believe me, it had nothing to do with "daylight saving time"!

My mother helped my father with this job. I was bundled up and placed in the wagon, first on one end, then on the other as the wagon filled up. The sound of ears hitting the "bang board" in the crisp air could be heard far away.

My father would look for "perfect ears" to save for next year's seed; hybrid corn hadn't been discovered yet. If he happened to see a rabbit, he'd hit it with an ear of corn and we'd have fresh meat for supper.

We'd fill one wagon in the morning, and while Father scooped the corn into the crib, Mother fixed our noon meal. There was no time for a big meal, which was called "dinner". Our evening meal was "supper", and now, at age 81, I still refer to meals this way. Dinner just doesn't seem like the evening meal to me.

After the noon meal, we'd go back and pick another load. When that one was scooped into the crib, we'd do the regular chores—slopping the hogs, milking and separating the milk. These things had

When the wagons were full of corn, it was time to take them back to the barnyard and scoop the ears into a crib.

to be done, no matter how tired your back was.

Farming still is hard work, but modern machinery and better methods have enabled American farmers to feed the hungry of the world. I'm glad that I can remember how we got here.

—*Esther Martin, Porter, Indiana*

Autumn has always been my favorite season, and my strongest memory of it stems from the October my dad used dried cornstalks to make an Indian tepee between the silo and the night pasture.

One of my mother's brass hanging planters became my cooking pot, and an old blanket became my bed. My dog and I practically lived in it all day. It was even better when my cousin came over. When we went to the tepee, a full moon was rising over the cornfields. We whooped and hollered like real Indians on the warpath.

Later, we'd settle down, and I'll never forget the peace and tranquillity of that moon and the soft conversation between my parents, who were milking. I wish everyone in the world could know just one evening like that—the closeness of God and family on a farm.

—*Janet Lawrence*
Grant Park, Illinois

Every fall, the pungent, tangy fragrance of cabbage working its way into sauerkraut filled the air in our cellar. Several tall crocks stood on the floor, with large rocks on top to prevent blowing during fermentation.

84

Outside the cellar, life bustled with activity as we prepared for the long cold winter ahead. This was the way it was growing up on a farm in the Midwest during the 1930's.

During butchering, our oven worked overtime, rendering lard from the meat. Every bit of meat that couldn't be canned or smoked had to be eaten while fresh; extra meat was shared with neighbors.

How I loved the smell of pork skin being rendered into cracklings! As they came out of the oven, I couldn't wait for them to cool and would usually burn my hands. We used the entire animal, making everything from headcheese to pickled pig's feet.

The final jobs of late summer were making soap and hominy and gathering hickory nuts. With rendered lard and lye, Mom made soap in a huge black kettle over a fire in the backyard. Hominy emerged from corn treated with lye to soften the kernels. I never understood the art of hominy making, but no one made hominy like my mother's! Hickory nuts were used for our cakes and chocolate fudge.

Today, I remember that special time in early November. With the urgent work of summer and fall finished, a calmness settled upon us—a hushed anticipation as we waited for winter to arrive.

—*Alice Loy Lange, Prescott, Arizona*

Mmy folks were always prepared for winter. Papa raised sorghum, which was made into black strap molasses, and also filled silos with wheat, corn, barley and oats for the chickens and livestock.

The cellar was filled with many provisions: the potatoes and several barrels of apples that we raised...100 pounds of cabbage we purchased from another farmer...a huge barrel of pickles put down in salt brine...and two 100-pound sacks of sugar.

We had no heat upstairs in the bedrooms, so we heated bricks, or rod irons that we used for ironing, and wrapped them in cloths so our bed would be warm.

We all wore long-handled underwear in the winter. Us girls also wore long black stockings and shoes that came up over our ankles, then overshoes over them. The overshoes were waterproof and had fleecy lining, so they kept feet fairly warm.

Washdays in winter were something else again. All that long underwear on the line would freeze stiff as a board; if the wind blew, it seemed like they all creaked. Mama had a washing machine with a handle that pushed back and forth with elbow grease. The water was warmed by a boiler set on two "eyes" of the wood-burning cookstove.

When the ice on the Solomon River got thick enough, Papa and a neighbor, Fred Jones, would get together and cut ice for the "icehouse", which was a large hole in the ground. The blocks of ice were put down with clean wheat straw. When the "house" was full, a roof was built over it, so we had ice all summer.

One winter day, a blizzard came up while my sister Dee Dee and I were at school. We had to stay with our grandmother in Woodston. Dee Dee and I got in a lot of coal and cut up some boxes Grand-

Doing laundry in the 1930's was hard work—even more so in winter.

85

ma had in her coal house for kindling. It was a good thing we did, for during the night, the snow piled on the front porch until you couldn't see there was a porch.

If it hadn't been for a neighbor, we couldn't have gotten out. He finally got over and shoveled us out. The snowdrifts were 20 feet high. When they dug out Woodston's main street, it was like driving through a tunnel. The snow was packed so hard you could walk on top of it. The kids gathered with their sleds and we slid up and down the drifts.

—*Ruth Smith, Woodston, Kansas*

When I was in eighth grade in the one-room Green School in northern Indiana, we advanced to an honest-to-goodness orange-colored school bus. Before that, a farmer or farmer's wife drove us to school in a touring car with side curtains, so riding in that magnificent new bus was a treat for us.

One December day that year, it began to snow around noon. We noticed the snow from our schoolroom windows, but didn't realize its proportions. When our new bus didn't come, we began to realize something serious was happening. The bus never made it that afternoon; the driver could not perform miracles—even with a new orange-colored bus.

As we waited, our teacher, Mr. Hostetler, led us in singing and playing games to keep us occupied and calm. But when it began to get dark, that didn't work anymore. The wind outside was blowing and howling, and the unsettled children were on the verge of howling, too.

The school had no electricity or telephone. Finally, Mr. Hostetler said he was going to the neighbors, Mr. and Mrs. Ora Anderson, to make some telephone calls for help. He said he would be back real soon, and that in the meantime, we should all stay inside the building.

One fifth grader said between tears that he had to go home, and if Mr. Hostetler did not let him go he would go downstairs and chop off his own head. Mr. Hostetler asked me to be in charge of the school while he was gone, and told me to keep Leonard out of the basement. That felt like a big responsibility with around 40 pupils, and I certainly was glad when he returned, and doubly glad that little Leonard had not lost his head.

The nearby farm families opened their homes to the children, and several farmers promised our teacher they would come with wagons or sleds to get all the children they could. So everyone was

Taking a motorized bus to school in rural Indiana in 1930 was a real treat for kids used to walking.

safe. We could literally identify with Whittier's poem *Snow Bound* for the next week or more. That was in the days before snowplows, so our world in that farming community stood still for the next week. —*D.J. Mishler, Goshen, Indiana*

Threshing crews made short work of mounds of food (left). Potato pickers (below) also worked up a hearty appetite; photo is from Chuck Halla, Hartford, Wisconsin.

I clearly remember threshing time on the farm. Two of the neighbors—brothers Mike and Orie Guthrie—had a threshing machine powered by an early 1930's Model D John Deere tractor.

To me, the most important part of the crew were the many wonderful farm women who put together these delicious meals. I never saw a farmer's wife who wasn't a good cook. That was one of those requirements of raising a family.

There is no way to explain the marvelous meals those women put on those tables. As a kid, when I looked around and saw all those big hungry men devouring all that food, it left room for only one main goal in my small mind—to get on that threshing crew! I wanted to put my feet under the table with those men in the worst way.

Now, there was always more than enough food left over for the women and kids after the men went back to work. But I figured if I could get on that threshing crew, I could get my feet under that table *every day* instead of just when they were threshing at our place.

After Dad saw his way clear to buy a pony from a neighbor for us kids, I thought I had it all figured out. The men out in the field pitching bundles always needed plenty of good drinking water. I was probably about 10 or 11 at this time, so I tried to

hire out as a water boy. I figured I'd carry two jugs of water on my pony and make the rounds, supplying plenty of good cool drinking water to all the haulers and pitchers.

I didn't care about pay—I just wanted around that table! But the idea didn't fly. Turned out all the bundle wagons already carried water jugs.

Dad always furnished a team and wagon to haul bundles to the threshing machine. I figured my next best shot was getting on that bundle wagon. But Dad told me I was too small to load and pitch bundles all day long. You see, Dad was very determined to carry his part of any load and wasn't about to send a kid out to pitch against those men.

My big break came the year I was 13. Dad didn't have his granaries ready, and the threshing crew was getting close to our place. So, one morning he asked me if I could handle the bundle wagon while he finished getting ready.

What an opportunity—of course, I could! Was I ever feeling grown up that morning when I got my team ready and headed down the road to where we were threshing. You can bet there wasn't a man on the crew that was going to outdo this kid.

I don't remember how long it took Dad to get ready to take his wagon back, but by that time, I had convinced him that I could handle the job. From that time on, it was my job to take care of my team and wagon and haul those bundles.

I turned on extra willpower when I got up to that dinner table. I think that's where I developed my great ability to eat. —*Vernon Landes*
Bartlesville, Oklahoma

My mother and I farmed about 50 acres of land in Ohio, 35 of which were planted to wheat. In 1940, the only threshing machine working in our area was owned by a relative.

When they came to our farm, the crew was short one man because that year, several of the young men from our area were volunteering for military service. So I was recruited for threshing work.

I fed the sheaves of wheat into the threshing machine. Boy, was that hot work! At the end of the day, the boss said I had worked as well as any of the men and asked Mom if I could accompany the crew for the rest of the season. He said he'd pay Mom for my work, and since

During harvesttime, even the ladies of the family were sometimes called upon to work in the fields.

J.C. Allen and Son

we sorely needed the money, she agreed. As you can guess, we worked hard and ate hearty as the farmers' wives put their tastiest victuals on the table for the threshing crews.

When the season was completed, the boss said I had been a good worker—for a 17-year-old girl!
—*Lynn Hall, La Mesa, California*

Igrew up on a farm near Waco, Nebraska during the 1920's and '30's. During the Great Depression, life wasn't easy in Kansas, Nebraska and the Dakotas.

I remember my father planting his crops and saying, "God willing, we'll have a harvest." Faith in the good Lord sustained him and other farmers. The crops, such as they were, began to be harvested in late June—first the oats, then barley, rye and spelts.

When the grain was cut and bound, shocking the bundles became a family affair. My sisters and brothers and I learned at an early age that a job was to be done well. We took pride in the fact that our grain shocks withstood rain and windstorms.

I really looked forward to the threshing season. When I was 13 years old, my father was unable to haul bundles from the field to the separator, so it became my job to fill in for him. It was hard work, but I soon learned to hold my end to keep the machine threshing the grain.

Soon my hands were blistered and raw. Underarm deodorant was unheard-of to soothe sore armpits. Instead, we used cornstarch to ease the soreness. The days were long, hot and hard.

It was a disgrace to arrive at the threshing machine

with half a load. In order for a load to stay on the bundle rack, the sides had to be carefully stacked and filled up the center, holding the bundles' heads in place. Barley straw was difficult to load, because it was slippery and would easily slide off the load. This was an embarrassment, and it happened several times to me until I learned the technique of good bundle loading.

The last day of threshing was a welcome event. The farmers were thankful for what the Good Lord had provided. It was also a time for them to think about next year's crop.

—*Darrell Naber*
Muskegon, Maine

When I was a child, I spent many holidays on my grandparents' farm just outside Portage, Wisconsin. It's a centennial farm (100 years in the same family) that was started by my grandfather's father.

I used to sit on top of the stock tank for hours, surveying the whole barnyard. But my most vivid memories relate to winter sleigh rides down through the fields.

Grandpa had a bobsled with box seats. He'd fill the sled with straw and then hitch up the team, old "Dick" and "Dan". For this time of year, Grandpa would put on the jingle-bell harness. Oh, the sound of those bells as the horses moved into a fast walk or trot—I can hear it yet!

It would be so cold that the snow would crunch under the runners and under the horses' hooves. Hundreds of stars would dot the sky and the horses would blow clouds of vapor.

Years later, after Grandpa died, my uncle or one of the boys would drive the team and we older kids would take care of the little ones. The sound of those bells was still the same!

—*Barbara Hodges*
Midland, Michigan

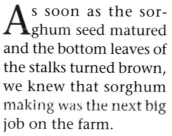

As soon as the sorghum seed matured and the bottom leaves of the stalks turned brown, we knew that sorghum making was the next big job on the farm.

Actually, I hated the chore of stripping cane; the leaves had sharp edges. But we also knew how exciting and fun it would be to see that cane juice cooked into sweet sorghum at the cane mill.

A mule turns a mill that presses the juice from sorghum stalks in 1918.

First, we stripped the mature leaves from the cane, from the seed head to the ground. Papa wanted no leaves left, even dead ones near the ground; they'd affect the color and taste of the syrup. Then we cut the stalks down at the ground. Two people worked at this job—one holding several stalks by the seed head while the other sliced the stalks off.

The stalks were laid in piles spaced several feet apart. Then we'd get down on our hands and knees to cut the seed heads from the stalk. A team followed with a two-horse wagon, loading the cane carefully from both sides of the wagon. Then it was off to the

89

syrup mill, where the cane was unloaded and fed into a grinder pulled by a mule in a circular motion. The juice was placed into a rectangular-shaped copper pan with partitions for the different stages of cooking.

A large fire was built under one end of the pan where the cooking started. As the juice slowly changed consistency, it flowed through the partitions, moving farther and farther from the fire.

The syrup-maker kept a close watch on the sorghum juice, making sure it was stirred properly and that the "skimming" was removed. When the syrup turned the right color and was the correct consistency, he'd call for the gallon jugs.

It was a toss-up as to which were more numerous—kids eating syrup skimming, or yellowjackets swarming around the skimming discarded in a nearby pit in the ground. Riding home in the wagon, loaded with enough syrup to last all winter and our stomachs "filled to the brim" with syrup skimming, we kids had mixed emotions about how much fun it was.

See, that sorghum syrup went well at breakfast with Mama's home-cooked biscuits and hotcakes smeared with good country butter. But our stomachs didn't feel so good because we had eaten so much syrup skimming.

—*Ernest Wester*
Smyrna, Georgia

How well I remember the threshing season on the farm! My most vivid memory concerns the fall I was 4 or 5 years old. At sunset, the men came into the house for the evening meal, including the man in charge of the steam engine that ran the threshing machine.

He was black with soot and sweat. And as he went by, he pinched my fat little cheeks and said he thought he would take me home with him. This scared me, so I hid behind a piece of furniture, falling asleep there.

When I couldn't be found, everyone went looking for me, searching pig and cattle pens and wells, hoping that I had not gotten into somebody's wagon. After a third search of the house, my mother finally found me. The engine man said he had surely learned a lesson.

—*Mildred Duffy*
Bella Vista, Arkansas

I grew up on a dairy farm in western New York, and one of my strongest memories involves the winter when I was 9.

Our farm was on a narrow country road, about a mile from the main highway. It was the 1940's,

A strong sense of satisfaction filled farmers' hearts when stacking hay bales.

and the winter that year was so severe that many a day the plows could only keep the main roads open.

In those days, milk was put in heavy 10-gallon cans and kept in a vat of ice water. Every other day, a big truck would come and take it to the processing plant. But during that awful winter, sometimes the only way the milk got to the truck was by horse-drawn bobsled, graciously provided by a neighboring dairy farmer.

He would travel wherever the least snow was and meet the truck at the highway. And during the planting and harvesting seasons, my father would help the neighbor in return—maybe lend him a piece of machinery, or help repair something, or give him some vegetables or fruit when we had more than we needed.

—Norma Morris
Varysburg, New York

Canning time at our farmhouse in the 1930's was kind of like a family reunion. My grandparents only lived about 4 miles away on another farm, so they'd come help my mother on canning day.

I would get up early on that special day and go to the garden to help pick the green beans or peas or gather the corn. Later in the morning, my grandparents would come. They'd sit in a circle, breaking beans or shelling peas with my mother and me—and even with Daddy and my older brother, if they weren't busy doing something else. We would sit on the back porch or in the big kitchen, depending on the weather.

We'd put old newspaper on our laps and heap on several handfuls of beans from the big baskets.

We'd break them and look for bad spots, talking and laughing while we worked. Often a bean would pop out of the shell and fly across the room, or maybe even hit someone in the circle, and we'd laugh about that, too.

The broken beans were put in a big dishpan, and when we'd get a pan full, Mother would usually stop and take the broken beans, start washing them and pack them in the clean canning jars, which she had washed the night before.

My grandparents also helped us seed cherries and peel peaches for canning. Those jobs were messy and sticky, and we'd laugh when the juice ran down our arms, or someone got a squirt in the face. I remember that quite often we laughed about our itching noses when we couldn't scratch them.

Cutting corn off the cob was a messy job, too, but it was worth it to eat that delicious yellow vegetable on a cold winter day. It was also a special treat to have those pretty peach halves or a cherry pie with a winter meal.

We had lots of fun "putting away" our produce, mainly because we all worked together to do it. It might benefit some families today if they could sit down in a circle, prepare produce for canning, and

J.C. Allen and Son

Food canned during the sweltering heat of summer would later taste mighty fine on a cold winter day.

laugh and talk. I believe the communication among our family was better than it is in the families nowadays. It was a special time that I looked forward to each year.

—*Lucille Stamper*
Danville, Indiana

The wonders of this age of technical machines often make the inventions of earlier times look pretty insignificant by comparison. But there were inventions of past years that must have seemed just as amazing then as any new computer does to us today.

The combine was one of those machines. As you pulled it through a field, it would cut standing grain and separate the seeds from the straw, all in one operation. This was a big improvement over the threshing machine, which stayed in one place while the farmer brought the grain to it on horse-drawn wagons.

Our first combine was a used one, as was every piece of farm equipment that we ever owned. It was operated by a power takeoff, which connected on the back of our little Case tractor. Instead of a bin to hold the grain, our combine had a wooden platform with a steel railing and a board seat.

A square pipe with two branched openings came down at one side of the platform. Under each opening was a place to hang two burlap bags. When one bag would become full of grain, we'd switch the grain flow to the other side, and the full bag was removed, tied and dropped down a ramp to the ground.

If the bag had not been tied securely, it would burst open when it hit the ground, spilling a good part of the grain.

Because I was too small to handle the heavy bags, we hired a teenage neighbor for the job. I can still see the fiery hair that framed his freckled cheeks, and the red puffy gums that showed around his white teeth as he grinned after pushing me off the wooden seat we were supposed to share.

Sometimes he would daydream and a bag would overfill. That would back grain up into the pipe and

Combines like this one, circa 1918, revolutionized the farming industry.

J.C. Allen and Son

make it almost impossible to switch the grain flow lever over to the other bag. This always caused the precious grain to spill, which didn't go over too well with my father, who at most other times had a very pleasant disposition.

At times, there was no teenage boy available to tend the bags, so I got the job. What an exciting time this was for me! I felt like the captain of a huge ship, riding alone on that wooden platform with the roar of the machine, the air full of dust and chaff, and grasshoppers and spittle bugs jumping everywhere.

When one bag was full, I would switch the lever to the empty bag and give Dad a wave when the second bag contained just the right amount of grain. Then he would stop the tractor, remove and tie the tops of both bags with a piece of twine and a special knot, slide them carefully to the ground and attach two empty bags under the pipes.

In the cool of the evening, after milking and supper were over, we would return to the field with the tractor and wagon to collect the fat bags. By the time every bag was on the wagon, it was usually dark for the trip back to the barn. I would ride at the back of the wagon with a grain bag for a seat and a flashlight close at hand in case a speeding car might come up suddenly from behind on the dirt road.

Parked next to one of today's self-propelled giant combines, our small machine of 40 years ago would be little more than a curiosity. But anyone who's ever ridden on that platform, chewing handfuls of fresh wheat into mouthfuls of pasty-tasting gum, or who has traveled home by moonlight on a wagon loaded with fresh-cut grain, realizes the satisfaction of a successful harvest doesn't come from just counting the number of acres you covered in a day.

—*Robert Wichterman*
Battle Creek, Michigan

Our farm in northeast Ohio was infested with bumblebees. One hot summer day at haying time, my dad told me to take our team of gray mares out to mow the clover field. I did just that. I was mowing along, doing a good job, when I came upon a nest of bumblebees.

They flew up in a swarm. I jumped off the mower—the horses went one way and I went another. When I realized what was happening, I took off after the runaway horses, screaming for them to stop.

Fortunately, they were old, and it didn't take long to persuade them to stop. The field was a big mess. I didn't tell my dad about the incident, but he could clearly see where I had missed mowing the clover, and when he got done raking, he asked me what had happened.

Fearing he'd be angry, I reminded him what had occurred the previous year when the same field was in wheat. We'd used the binder to cut the wheat, then shocked it. The shocks were out there for a few weeks, and a swarm of bees took refuge in one of them.

I was pitching bundles up to him on the hay wagon, and when I pitched this particular shock, the bees went with it. Dad slid down the side of the wagonload of wheat and took off running. I went the other way. I'll never forget it.

—*Charles Coxson*
Warren, Ohio

Julie Habel

Larsh Bristol

Julie Habel

Tom Narwid

Tom Narwid

Spring on the farm means frolicking in wildflowers (inset above). Continuing clockwise: misty morning at North Hartland, Vermont; cows near Bradford, Vermont; tractor ready for spring planting in Iowa; interesting field geometry. Opposite page: placid farm scene in Vermont; inset, soft beauty inside harsh barbed wire.

Anthony Beaverson

Rick Miller

Julie Habel

Terry Donnelly

Summer in the country means serene fields and farm buildings bathed in evening light (above). Continuing clockwise: cornfield and angular barn in Brown County, Wisconsin; farm girl and wildflowers silhouetted by sunset; Midwest farmer checks grain for harvest; hay bales dot the horizon near Traverse City, Michigan.

Darryl R. Beers

Friendly sunflowers follow the August sun near Kendall, Wisconsin (below). Continuing clockwise: Guernsey cow making friends; checking the crops; farm silhouette in Lancaster County, Pennsylvania.

Mount Burns

Doyle Yoder

Bob Clemenz; inset, Rick Miller

G. Alan Nelson

98

Mary Lisburg

Dick Dietrich

Fall's arrived on farm near Locust Lake in Pennsylvania's Schuykill County (above); inset, young girl holds bundle of grain in rural North Dakota. Opposite page, clockwise from top right: autumn means brilliant foliage in Washington County, Minnesota; farm amid fall colors near Peacham, Vermont; Trail, Ohio countryside; combining outside Pendleton, Oregon; harvesting corn near Janesville, Wisconsin.

Dick Dietrich

Julie Habel

Julie Habel

Julie Habel

Julie Habel

Though it's winter, outdoor work doesn't stop on Iowa farm (above). Continuing clockwise: cows huddle in the cold...so does family; pretty farm at East Orange, Vermont; tractor waits out snowstorm. Opposite page: peaceful winter scene near Fletcher, Vermont; inset, chicken tries to find a warm perch.

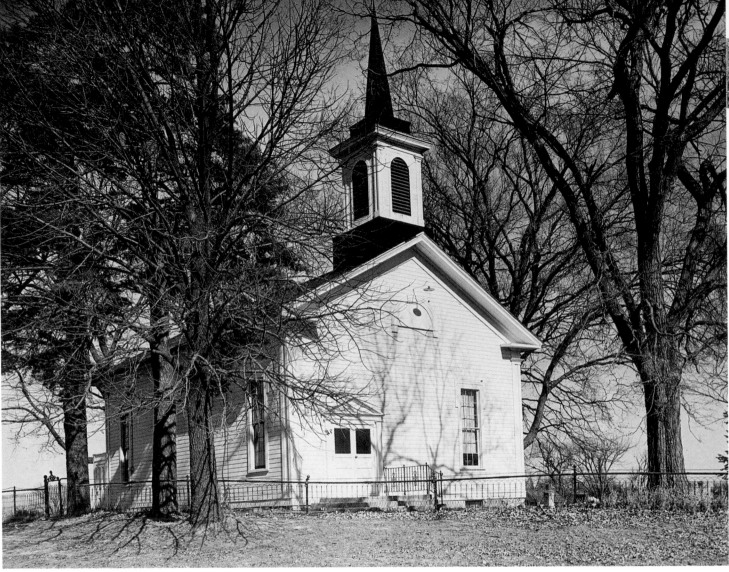

When I was growing up in the 1920's in central Nebraska, religion was as much a part of our lives as eating and sleeping.

We practiced the Golden Rule and kept our faith as a matter of everyday principle, but we had very few formal church services. There was no country church in that particular community, so the services we did have were held in a one-room schoolhouse.

There was a bigger parish in a nearby town, and ministers of numerous faiths visited our community at regular intervals. Usually the service was held during the summer on Sunday evenings.

One of these faithful preachers was a minister who rode a motorcycle. You always knew when he was within a few miles because of the noise from his old 1920's-vintage Harley-Davidson motorcycle. It was dependable transportation, inexpensive to operate (with gasoline at 20¢ a gallon) and on warm summer evenings, it was a pleasant ride to the different parishes.

As a small child, I was almost in awe of the noisy olive-green machine. I'd hang on tight to Mama's hand as the minister arrived in a cloud of dust. He was a tall man who always wore khaki riding breeches, high brown leather boots, a leather cap with goggles and a bombardier jacket. As he strode across the school yard, he looked like something completely foreign to my farm-oriented young mind.

But when he removed his jacket and cap and read scripture and verse from the old King James Version of the Bible at the front of the one-room school, he kept our attention completely. He was not a "fire and brimstone" preacher; he talked softly of the love and forgiveness we could expect from our heavenly Father.

There was a piano at the school, and usually someone in the congregation could play those old familiar hymns. Occasionally, some visiting soloists came. There were two sisters who were exact replicas of Kate Smith, and their voices were equally as exhilarating. They would sing *The Old Rugged Cross*, *The Little Brown Church in the Vale* and *In the Garden* until their faces were drenched with perspiration. But they enjoyed the message in their music so much that they were always prepared to sing more.

We'd pass a hat to take up a collection for the Harley-riding minister, but I doubt if he ever received enough for his trouble. These were hard times, soon after the first World War, and the struggling farmers eked out a bare existence on their farms.

After the service was over and the last hymn had been sung, the minister would roar away into the

A motorcycle similar to this one brought a minister and his words of salvation to some central-Nebraska parishes in the 1920's.

darkness on his motorcycle. We'd turn out the kerosene lights in the school and shut the door—locks were unheard-of as well as unnecessary.

Today, we can listen to ministers on the radio and watch complete church services with 50-voice choirs on television. But none can quite compare to that traveling preacher on a Harley who brought us the message of salvation. —*Kathryn McGaughey*
Denver, Colorado

In his early teen years, my older brother decided to hang a gunnysack for Santa to fill, instead of his stocking, which was smaller than mine. The next morning, he found it full of corncobs!
—*Ruby Schechter, Davison, Michigan*

My grandparents lived on a farm outside of Millersview, Texas. Grandmother strongly believed in the Bible, particularly the Ten Commandments. So it wasn't surprising that one Sunday afternoon she refused to repair some cotton sacks that my granddad needed to use on Monday morning; she said she couldn't work on a Sunday.

But Granddad kept pestering her, so she finally said she'd fix them. However, she also told him that if she did, he wasn't going to be able to work the next day.

The next morning, when Granddad got up to go out and pick cotton, it was raining. It rained for an entire week, which is a lot of rain in that part of Texas. Grandmother told him he should have nev-

er asked her to work on Sunday. And he never did again!
—*Cindy Rives, Midland, Texas*

Several years ago, my husband, Don, and I planted about 150 good-sized tomato plants on our 9-acre place.

The next day, I went out in the late afternoon to look at them. The weather had suddenly turned cool and a wind began to blow. I looked up at the southern sky and saw the clouds were black and ugly—a storm was coming.

I had nothing to protect that many plants from hail or rain. So I just looked up to God and said, "You'll have to take care of my tomato plants. I can't, but I know You can." I felt a few pings of hail as I walked to the house.

Later that evening, my husband and I drove into town, less than a mile away. We could hardly believe our eyes. While almost no hail at all had fallen at our house, about *6 inches of hail* covered virtually everything else—it looked like Christmas in June. The berry crops in the area were ruined. I felt very grateful to God for answering my prayer.

That made me think of another true story told by my grandparents about a hailstorm. They lived in Kansas on a wheat farm, and my grandma was a real Christian woman and trusted in God.

One day an insurance peddler came through their area, selling insurance against "acts of God". To say the least, she was a little shook up at the offer. She simply said, "No! We will trust in God. He will take care of us and the crops."

Upon hearing of her decision, the neighbors

didn't think she was very wise. Soon a storm came and you could hear the roar of hail. Grandma realized she was being put to the test. She dropped to her knees and prayed. God heard her prayers.

When the storm was over, they went out to survey the damage. The hail had flattened everyone's wheat—except for my grandparents'! Theirs stood straight and tall, with the hail piled up high around the fence line. They celebrated with thankful hearts and used the hailstones to make a treat of homemade ice cream.   —*Bonnie Morse, Portland, Oregon*

We never celebrated Thanksgiving as such, but that's not to say we weren't thankful. I remember spending many Thanksgivings in the barn stripping tobacco. I assumed every other kid from school was doing the same thing—and most of them probably were. By the end of the day, I wasn't too thankful to be out of school. It was hard work stripping "tips"!

But the time passed quickly. We usually brought the radio, and Dad would sing along with every song he knew, and hum or whistle along with the ones he didn't. If we had other work hands helping, they entertained us. Dad always teased everybody. We passed around a lot of tall tales and jokes. Dad told the punch lines at least twice if they were especially funny.

The best part of the day was dinnertime. By noon, we were really thankful for bologna sandwiches and moon pies. We were always poor, but I didn't know it. I never missed a meal, although I did get tired of "beans and taters". Mom kept it bearable by fixing different desserts every day, everything from blackberry or peach cobbler to a simple biscuit pudding.

Bologna was a treat back then. I heard Mom say many times we should be thankful for our bologna sandwiches. That's why I fondly think of Thanksgiving Day as Bologna Day.   —*Carolyn Bertram Monticello, Kentucky*

Our country church was definitely the center of our farming community.

I fondly remember the summer ice cream socials that took place on farmyards. The men visited and

Church dinners were often the center of social activities in small rural communities.

hand-cranked (or plugged in) the ice cream freezers by the barn. While the ice cream was freezing, we children played with relatives, distant cousins and neighbors. The women visited and set out other goodies.

In my memory, it was quite a lineup of freezers! It was difficult to choose which concoctions to sample: peach, strawberry, cherry, maple, coffee, chocolate chip, chocolate and lots of vanillas. No ice cream store could compete with the taste of a country church ice cream social.

In the days when a few cows automatically went with farming, an ice cream freezer was a household necessity! Above all, I really treasured the close bond we had worshiping and sharing fellowship together.
—*LeAnn Gossen, Corn, Oklahoma*

I'll always treasure the Christmas of 1932. I was 8 years old, one of 11 children living on a farm just outside of Nashua, Minnesota. My parents were struggling to hold on to their farm in the midst of the Great Depression.

With Christmas approaching, our mother told us not to expect any toys from Santa—we couldn't even afford a tree. We knew our parents were hard-pressed to feed 11 of us—ages 6 months to 16 years—so we already knew the holidays would be somewhat bleak.

Christmases in the 1930's were short on gifts but long on family love.

Just 2 days before Christmas, one of my older brothers and I were walking to school with some neighboring children. Just as we crossed the railroad tracks entering town, we saw a truck loaded with Christmas trees crossing the tracks, its load bouncing up and down.

I said to my brother, "I wish one of those trees would fall off that truck." Believe it or not, at that very instant, three or four of those trees fell off! The driver never noticed and kept on going. I picked up one large tree, which was about 8 to 10 feet tall. We were happy to at least have a Christmas tree.

On Christmas Eve, our parents loaded all of us into our 1915 Dodge car and drove 20 miles to the little town of Doran. There Santa appeared in the town square with a sack of candy for each child. There also were other prizes awarded for various things. We won a sack of flour for having the oldest car, and we tied with another family of 11 children for having the largest family. We split that prize—a ton of coal—with them.

We awoke on Christmas to find a present for each of us under the tree. I got a full-size wagon, all made of wood. My younger brother got a wheelbarrow, a younger sister got a doll bed and so on. We children finally realized why we weren't allowed in the basement for several weeks prior to Christmas—Dad was busy building toys.

We also realized how much our dad and mother had sacrificed for us. We may have been very poor, but their love made us feel rich, indeed!
—*Bart Schoenecker, Sedgwick, Kansas*

The Lord always provides, and I have a story to prove it.

My husband, Oscar, and I were high school sweethearts in Sawyer, North Dakota. We graduated in 1926 and were married the spring of 1929. By 1934, we had three children, Delores "Sis", Kenneth "Bud" and baby Kathlyn "Kitty".

We lived on a couple of different farms and always had milk cows, chickens and a garden. Times were tough; I remember cream getting down to 11¢ per pound of butterfat, eggs costing 6¢ a dozen and postage stamps going for 2¢. Sometimes we didn't have 2¢!

We moved onto a farm with a big square house, a cellar under the kitchen and nothing modern—no electricity then. It gave us more room, but when the earth froze and the cold winds blew, it was a challenge to the old coal-burning heating stove and cook stove to keep us comfortable.

There was always a period of getting cold, even though we fired the stove at night. We took our best bedding and put it on Sis and Bud, who slept on an old daybed, one at each end. And we had blankets for Kitty in the reed baby buggy. We used our coats and jackets for our bed.

Now, the Ladies' Aid at St. Cecelia's Catholic Church in Velva held an annual bazaar with a good dinner, fancy work, goods for sale, a homemade wool-filled comforter for a door prize and, of course, bingo. We could all go for $2. After dinner, a neighbor man invited us to play a game of bingo at 10¢ a chance.

Wouldn't you know it, I won and chose a colorful Indian blanket. And when they announced the winner of the door prize, it was me again, so we had a comforter. We went home thanking our Creator for the wonderful gifts of the day.

We hung up our coats and jackets and put the warm blankets on our bed. The Indian blanket wore out in time, but we still have the comforter. It has been recovered several times, and we still use it on one of our spare beds.
—*Marcella Johnson*
Velva, North Dakota

My twin sister and I were 7 years old when we had our first communion.

Our aunt and grandma had made us pretty white dresses and veils. Seeing our pictures, you'd think we were precious little angels. By that afternoon, we were far from that!

Mom and Dad had bought both of us white sandals. We decided we wanted slip-on shoes instead, like our Uncle James had. So we took the sharpest paring knife out to the orchard and cut off our sandal straps.

I can't recall the outcome, but I'm certain Mom and Dad learned to take us along shopping! I know we learned a few valuable lessons—including how to be thankful for what you receive.

As we recall this incident, we know now the hardship two more pairs of shoes must have been.
—*Martha Sheehy, Perry, Iowa*

Mary (Hoag) Trimble of Berryville, Arkansas celebrated her first communion the same day her brother, Don, was confirmed in 1936 in Marshfield, Wisconsin.

We only got boiled eggs once a year, and that was at Easter. Back then, eggs were as good as money; you could trade them for groceries at the store. Many times, as soon as the hens laid eggs, Mama would send one of us to the store to get one egg worth of sugar and one egg worth of coffee.

So Easter was a happy time; we got a few eggs to boil and color and put in our homemade baskets,

Dyeing eggs always made Easter a memorable holiday.

which consisted of small square boxes covered with some kind of paper, and handles made of wire covered with crepe paper.

To color the eggs, we would find scraps of faded material and dip them in hot water so the colors could run. Then we'd let the water cool before dipping our eggs in them.
—*Mrs. Marcus Bonds*
Gloster, Mississippi

The most precious gift given to me by my parents was my introduction into the Christian faith.

Since I grew up in a community of people of German descent near Frankfort, Illinois, many of the residents were relatives of mine, as well as members of the Lutheran church. As children, we attended the Lutheran grade school for 8 years. Each spring, we practiced songs and skits to perform at the annual church picnic.

The picnic was held on the Fourth of July. It was an all-day affair held on the grounds between the church and the school. When the program was about to begin, the women stopped assembling tables and tables of food, and the men temporarily stepped away from the beverage stand.

Children quit playing softball and horseshoes, and everyone congregated on the chairs assembled in front of the makeshift stage. The performance began with the Pledge of Allegiance and ended with the whole group singing *America the Beautiful.*

At the time, I didn't appreciate the significance of celebrating our country's birthday as well as our re-

ligious freedom. Those church picnics bring back memories of events that are part of my German heritage, celebrated in a country that accepts all beliefs.
—*Marilyn Bartels Johnson, Springfield, Missouri*

Our hog was real sick, so a fine Christian neighbor, Mr. Brooks, came by to look at her.

The hog had not gotten up for days. The neighbor asked Daddy if he wanted him to pray for the hog, and Daddy said, "Yes, if you want to." Well, before Mr. Brooks was finished praying, the hog got up, grunted and got well.

My family had always believed in miracles, but this was one of the greatest we'd seen in a while. Mr. Brooks helped his neighbors any way he could, but this helping hand was extra special.
—*Marlene Whitmire, Greer, South Carolina*

Shortly after Thanksgiving, Santa Claus would make an appearance at our house. The four of us kids would be in the living room with Mom, and all of a sudden, there'd be a loud knock at the door. The door would open and a hand wearing a black glove with thick white fur would come from around the corner and throw in a handful of nuts.

This would happen three or four times before Christmas. One evening, one of the nuts bounced off the table and hit Mom right in the eye. The next day, the younger ones told everyone how Santa had given Mom a black eye!

One strange thing, though: Dad never got to see

Santa. He was always in the basement putting coal in the furnace...

—Patricia Bromley
Canonsburg, Pennsylvania

Whenever I hear the hymn *Church in the Wildwood*, I think of our little country church, Fairhaven Baptist, which was about 3 miles from our home in rural Nebraska.

The congregation was small—an attendance of 40 was a big day—and most of them were my relatives, either actual uncles, aunts and cousins, or those of the "shirttail" variety. One of our family's favorite pastimes was figuring out how we might be related to someone in the community, and we usually could find some connection through several marriages.

One of the pillars of the church was Mr. Claude Smith, a majestic gentleman with white hair and an enormous white mustache. Some men in the back row might have dozed during a sermon, but never Mr. Smith. I used to think that if he believed in the Bible, it *must* be true. It wouldn't dare not be!

All the Sunday school classes met in one room. A stage divided by curtains formed two classes, one for small children and the other for grade-schoolers. A high school class, a young people's class and a Bible class shared the rest of the room.

As soon as you finished high school, you were promoted to the young people's class and remained there until you married. Then you automatically joined the Bible class. Age made no difference. If you never married, you always stayed in the young people's class.

The Tower of Babel had nothing on Fairhaven Sunday school. When everyone was talking at once, you could hardly hear what was being said. Years later, they added a basement and divided the vestibule so that every class had its own room.

One summer during church, a grasshopper got down my neck. Did you ever have a grasshopper inside your dress? Not only do their legs prickle you, but they spit "tobacco juice" and stain your clothes.

I didn't dare squirm or I would get one of Mother's "hard looks". So I sat all through the sermon clutching my dress so that grasshopper couldn't crawl around with its prickly legs.

Country churches like this one were often the spiritual beacon of a farm community. Photo taken by Hope Berge of Hagen, Saskatchewan.

Once a family of skunks made their home under the building, and the air in the church was pretty fragrant until the men trapped them for bounty. They donated the money to the Ladies' Aid.

Fairhaven Church is still there, and when I return home to Nebraska for a visit, I'm always welcomed as though I've never been away. I feel closer to God in that little church than anywhere else in the world.

—Rachael McKeag
Seattle, Washington

The Fourth of July was a special occasion for my family. We always held a large family reunion at

Grandpa's farm, and it was the only time each year when the whole family came together.

Grandma would have tables decked out with red-and-white checked tablecloths. There was so much food, it was unbelievable—a child's dream! There was a fresh watermelon in the watering trough, which was filled with ice for that special day. The watermelon was always a tasty treat on a hot day and provided the only time when it was okay to spit.

While the adults talked and reminisced, the children would scurry off for a day of great fun. Recreation included swinging as high as possible on the giant swing in the big oak tree. Whoever could touch the leaves with their feet was the "winner" (of course, it helped if you were older and had very long legs!).

The barn had two haymows, with a large section for storage in between. Around that time of year, the haymows weren't quite full yet, but there was still plenty of hay in which to make tunnels. The boys would pride themselves on making the longest, curviest, scariest tunnels. Sometimes it would take 20 minutes or more to crawl our way through the pitch-blackness of those tunnels.

When we'd get tired of that, Grandpa would allow us to take several ears of corn so we could hold "corn fights" across the facing haymows.

There also was a large rope swing in the center of the barn. A big knot served as the seat, and to mount it, you had to walk "tightrope" style halfway across a big beam—pretty scary sometimes! But the ride was well worth it. Why, with a good push, you could swing clear outside the huge barn doors! Today, most parents would consider it too dangerous. But it gave me many a thrill—and many a memory.

Then there were wheelbarrow races, with uncles loading up one of their nieces or nephews and racing wildly across the lawn. When we got too hot, we'd head for the creek to wade, splash and catch salamanders and crawdads. Toward the end of the day, Grandpa would get out his tractor and hay wagon for a big hayride.

To top it all off, we would walk about a mile down the road to a neighbor's place. He was born on the Fourth of July and shared fireworks in honor of his birthday. The sparklers in our hands and a glow in the sky signaled the end of the day—much too soon for our taste!
—*Bonnie Fisher, Amlin, Ohio*

After Christmas, the next most-anticipated holiday in our area was Easter. To us children, Easter Sunday was the start of spring. We knew good things, like going barefoot and no more "long handles", would soon follow.

Easter Sunday in 1940 dawned cloudy and cool, but this didn't dim our anticipation. At 9:30 a.m., all four of us, each carrying three boiled eggs, walked to church. The elders there pooled everyone's eggs for an egg hunt.

But Mother Nature had different ideas. Shortly after we arrived, it began snowing. In less than an hour, 2 inches of snow had fallen. By the time the storm ended, some 8 to 10 inches fell, although most of it melted overnight, as spring snow usually does.

The Easter when we had snowball fights instead

Patriotic fervor ran high in the early 1900's. Jean Taylor of Herrin, Illinois sent the photo; that's her mother, Alice Johns Daulby, second from left.

of an egg hunt was a memorable one. Easter fell on March 24 that year; snow at this late date was unusual.

—*Auton Miller, Piney Flats, Tennessee*

The Lone Pine Baptist Church has been a key part of my life since 1926. At first, it was a small one-room building with windows, but no screens. Often wasps would drift through the open windows and dart about on the ceiling. I was always afraid of them.

But wasps weren't the only things that found their way into the church. One Sunday during worship service, a bird flew in a window and hit the wall on the other side. After circling around the preacher sev-

eral times, it found an open window and departed.

Then there was the time the organist started playing the old pump organ and we heard an awful screaming. Some cats had wandered in through an open door and settled down in the organ. As the organist pumped, she mashed the cats. Ouch!

—*Verna Ray Humphrey, Palestine, Texas*

My brothers and I all attended public schools. But when school ended in April (this was the 1920's and '30's), we'd join the children at Holy Guardian Angels School in Cedar Grove, Indiana for religious instruction the entire month of May.

We'd ride to town, 5 miles away, in a milk truck

Numerous playground activities kept schoolchildren entertained during the '30s.

driven by my cousin. I was allowed to ride up front because I was a girl; the others had to ride in back with the milk cans. It was a rough ride for them, but much better than the walk home in the afternoon.

We walked in all kind of weather. Sometimes it was so hot and dusty that the walk seemed to take forever. The hot winds blew dust across the fields as the horses pulled disks to cultivate the endless brown fields. At other times, it was so cold that our fingers just about froze while carrying our lunch pails. Sometimes we would even see snow in the early part of May.

Our days of instruction were not all study. The school and church grounds were beautifully mowed and weeded by the boys. We girls swept walks and picked up any paper that dared to fall to the ground under the watchful eye of Father Clever. We swept and dusted the schoolrooms and cleaned and scrubbed the church until it sparkled.

We had swings, teeter-totters and wagon-wheel merry-go-rounds, all painted a patriotic red, white and blue. We played "dare base", "button button", "upset the fruit basket", "statues", "little Sally saucer", "may I" and many other games. We also played baseball with the boys if Father Clever had gone to Brookville.

The final day of instruction was a day to remember, with plenty of fun and games and Father Clever in a benevolent mood. We ran races around the graveyard, and the winner was rewarded with a penny. There were other contests, too. After the games were over came the most wonderful treat of all—tubs of French Bauer ice cream. Never was a treat so wonderful!

We really didn't believe that anything could add to our pleasure, but just as we were about to go home, out came a box of Cracker Jack for each child. Every box had a prize, but the one I treasured most was a ring with a beautiful red setting. My finger soon turned green, but our happiness was complete. We'd discovered that Father Clever was not the gruff old ogre he pretended to be.

Those days gave us many things—lasting friendships, a good foundation in our religious beliefs and a sense of responsibility in taking care of the community around us.　—*Dorothy Doerflein Levermann*
Highland Heights, Kentucky

The day my children were baptized was an important event. The minister held a special service for our family, as there were nine children—all cousins—being baptized at one time.

It was an impressive ceremony. All the devoted parents felt the importance of dedicating their children to God and wanting to bring them up with good morals in stable Christian backgrounds.

After the service, we held a potluck dinner, inviting the minister to join us. Each family brought their favorite dish, and mine was my family's favorite—ham and noodle casserole. I still remember Reverend Meyer enjoying the food. As he went back for seconds, he said, "Who made this ham and noodle dish? This is good!"

I seldom make this favorite dish without remembering Reverend Meyer, who was a dear friend. He is gone now, but I have many memories of him, plus much knowledge and philosophy gained from his sermons. Just knowing him as a friend was a

great privilege, and having him baptize our children made us especially grateful to him.   —*Irene Dunn, Hope, Idaho*

I remember all holidays well, but the one I liked best was the Fourth of July. Every family in the community would get together. The women would cook up a storm, and the men would go in a nearby creek and use only their hands to catch large catfish that lay submerged around tree trunks.

We always had plenty of fried chicken and other meats, just in case the men didn't catch any fish. But they usually caught enough, and we'd dress and cook them in a big black kettle, just like the one they used to render lard at hog-butchering time.

Later, we'd swim in the creek and get so sunburned we'd have blisters. Then we'd stuff ourselves with homemade ice cream. I remember when we'd get home, we'd take some cream off the milk and put it on our sunburn. You'd think we'd learn our lesson, but it happened every year.

—*Mazie Goodman, Dallas, Texas*

A Christmas Eve snowstorm made for a most memorable holiday when I was 6 years old, living on a farm in a German community in northeastern Indiana.

Most of our activities centered around the Lutheran church in our community, a tall white building

Farm women proudly unfurl the red, white and blue during a Fourth of July celebration.

with a bell tower, and Christmas Eve was no exception. On this day, we were to attend a traditional children's program at the church.

But in the afternoon, it had started to snow, and it continued to blow and drift into the early evening. We got about a half mile down the road in our 1925 Chevrolet when we saw our neighbor's car stuck in a snowdrift. They were too stuck to budge, so they all climbed into our car, and we returned to our farm.

There was a buggy in our barn that hadn't been used much since we bought our car, but it sure came in handy that night. Dad hitched up "Prince", his favorite horse, and all of us piled in and covered up with a big black horse blanket. It was warm but very prickly.

When we arrived at church, the grown-ups went in to take their place in the pews—men on the left side and women on the right. All the children gathered in the basement and prepared for the program.

Each of us held a candle to light our way. We walked, two by two, up the stairs and through the

two doors into the sanctuary, where it was dark except for the giant Christmas tree in the front of the church. The tree was decorated with shiny bulbs and icicles glittering from the lights of at least a hundred candles. As we marched in, singing *Heiligen Weihnachten*, we felt like Dorothy must have as she entered the Emerald City.   —*Regina Wise*
Dayton, Ohio

In October 1832 or September 1833 (the records differ), a man named Hugh Bowles organized a church in a grove about 10 miles southwest of Clinton, Illinois, with 17 charter members.

The families represented were probably former members of the Cane Ridge Meeting House in Bourbon County, Kentucky, well-known in the history of the Christian Church (Disciples of Christ). The first meetings were held in the grove or the members' log homes. In 1838, a log chapel known as the Union Church was erected to be used by Baptists and Methodists, as well as the folks from Cane Ridge.

In 1864, a frame building was erected for the Disciples only. It cost $3,000 and seated 600 people, and was the first Christian church in DeWitt County.

When the railroads and the towns of Midland City and Hallsville were built, many members decided houses of worship should be located in these towns. So, on July 30, 1887, about 100 people signed a charter establishing a church at Hallsville. A building was erected with no basement, although one was added in 1924.

Decades passed and times changed. When Hallsville's elementary school closed, interest moved to Clinton, the county seat. Older members passed away, attendance dropped, finances became a problem and the church doors closed in October 1971.

However, this was not the end for the historic church. In March 1980, a group of interested people drove out the pigeons, mended windows and weatherboarding and scrubbed for many hours.

On Easter Sunday in 1980, 126 people attended a worship service. The original pews, a piano and several large wooden folding tables were yet in the building. The pulpit furniture and other equipment were slowly being returned from a neighboring congregation.

On May 25, 1980, a rededication ser-

The Hallsville Christian Church near Clinton, Illinois marked its 100th birthday in 1987.

vice was attended by a large group of members and friends. Since then, extensive repairs have been made to the property, including metal siding, storm windows and doors and indoor rest rooms.

Services and Bible classes are held regularly. Hallsville Church has started its second 100 years.
—*Harriet Griffin, Clinton, Illinois*

Our local church was an integral part of life for Ma and Pa (my grandparents), and they didn't leave it behind on Sunday, either! I'm grateful to them for the legacy of faith they handed down.

Every Sunday morning without fail, we were scrubbed and curled and dressed in our best. We sang the old songs of faith together. Sometimes we were less than melodious, but the Lord says to "make a joyful noise"—so we did. Lifting voices together lifts spirits, too! Pa always sat in the "amen corner" with the other men, while we ladies occupied the other pews.

After the preacher opened the Holy Book for us with a rousing sermon, all were invited to "extend a hand of fellowship". As we sang a song, we gathered in a circle at the front by the "mourner's bench". I have special memories of this moment of shaking hands and hugs—the bonding of lives together.

In the summer months, many of the "sister" Baptist churches in the area would take turns having revival meetings. Although fieldwork was long and tiring, Pa would often travel several miles in the evening to attend a revival. It was my great joy to accompany him. On these occasions, my cousins and I enjoyed the lofty privilege of sitting with Pa

in the "amen corner". Many years later, the sounds and sights of praise, prayer and preaching still march through the halls of my memory.

I recall many beloved preachers from my childhood. How I loved and revered these good men. Very often my family had the preacher for Sunday

Dressing up in their Sunday best for church was a real treat for these rural Indiana women.

dinner. So I had the great privilege of learning that God's men are clothed in flesh like the rest of us. I remember these men as earnest, good, kind, loving and giving. I am indebted to them for their teaching and example.
—*Rose Shepherd*
West Union, West Virginia

Christmas was a special time on the farm for our family, marked by wonderful meals and desserts. Weeks before Christmas, we'd bake a fruitcake and a date nut cake. Closer to Christmas, we would bake molasses and sugar cookies. And about 2 weeks before Christmas, we butchered hogs and cows, from which we made bacon, ham and all different kinds of sausage.

On the morning of Christmas Eve, my mother would bake her famous sourdough coffee cake, and my oldest brother would go out and shoot a turkey for dinner. It was prepared immediately and placed in the stove to begin baking. It would be taken out that evening and put back in the next morning to finish baking.

In the afternoon, my mother, one of my sisters and I would go into the pasture and cut down a Christmas tree. Sometime after that, around dusk, Santa Claus came to decorate the tree and leave the presents. By family tradition, these gifts were opened on Christmas Eve. Each young child received one toy, a homemade dress or shirt and a writing tablet. The older children normally received only a dress or shirt.

On Christmas morning, after doing our chores, we drove to town and went to church. After church, we went home to prepare the Christmas dinner. My older brothers and sisters who were already married would stop by with their families to celebrate with us.   —*Alma Eckert Pehl, Fredericksburg, Texas*

The country church that I attended until a few years ago celebrated its 200th birthday in 1991. It was founded long before the county in which it's located.

In these early days in upper South Carolina, the settlers saw the need for a church. Ten people came

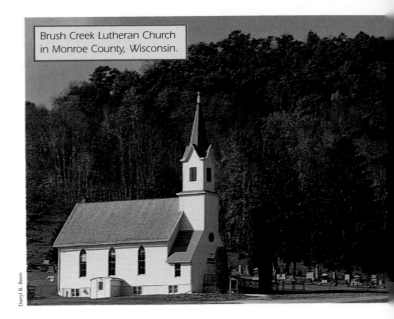

Brush Creek Lutheran Church in Monroe County, Wisconsin.

Darryl R. Beers

together in 1791 to organize the Brush Creek Church, later known as the Mount Pisgah Baptist Church.

From then until 1824, they met under a brush arbor or in a small cabin. In 1824, they built a more permanent building that served the young community until after the Civil War.

As a child growing up in the church, I have wonderful memories of Vacation Bible School, "Sunbeams", girls' auxiliary, day camps, retreats, socials and church services. It was at one of the socials that I met the young man who would later become my husband. We were married at this church and, in 1985, his funeral was held there.

The church and its close-knit congregation were our pillar of strength during his illness. He had been injured in a tree cutting accident and lived 69 days in the trauma unit of the local hospital. During those dark days, friends from the church were there daily to support and comfort me and my son and daughter. Their prayers, visits, cards, gifts of food and just their presence will always be etched in my mind and heart.

Large city churches have many various programs, but the small country church gives its members a special kind of care they so often need.

—*Jo Ann Wigington*
Hilton Head Island, South Carolina

Providing for Christmas on a homestead during the Depression was a monumental task. In 1931, my parents, Floyd and Pansy King, had just homesteaded land on the California-Oregon border. Like most families with small children, they worried about what they could do to make Christmas Day special.

Dad had $5, so he decided to take me and my sisters to town and see what he could find. He hitched up his team to the wagon, as the roads were too muddy for a car. But even the poor horses gave out before they had gone a mile, so he sent us disappointed girls home with the horses.

Taking a flour sack, he walked 6 miles up the railroad track that bordered the homestead, to the small town of Malin. It was late in the day before he returned home, the big sack filled with groceries and other things.

On Christmas morning, Mom and us girls found he had bought enough material to make an apron for each of them. A special treat was a sack of candy. Perhaps these were small gifts according to present-day abundance, but they represented a large sacrifice on Dad's part. It was a long-remembered Christmas, because when one has so little, anything can mean a lot.

—*Shirley Petersen*
Springfield, Oregon

While I never had the privilege of living on a farm, I did live amid farms and farming people from the early 1920's to the early 1940's. My dad was a Methodist preacher, so I grew up in country parsonages, which, along with churches, were the center of rural community activities.

Dad usually preached at four or five small churches scattered over a 50- to 100-square-mile area. The parsonages we lived in were under the auspices of the Central Texas Conference of the Methodist Church, but maintained by the local congregations. So people in the communities naturally had a proprietary interest in their parsonage.

In fact, because the parsonage ordinarily was next door to the church most centrally located in the preacher's circuit, many people considered it an extension of the church and, as such, public property. So our parsonage was a noisy place, filled with Mom's dish clattering, the kids' door banging and Dad's hymn singing, not to mention the constant coming and going of people needing all kinds of things.

On Sundays, they would come to use our bathroom if we had one and the church didn't. People would also come to discuss church business...complain about the song leader...praise the Sunday school teacher...get married...see if their cast-off furniture still had a place of honor in the living room...pray over problems...report emergen-

Country preachers like Joseph Horst Nissley were fixtures in rural communities. Photo's from grandson Clair Nissley, Middletown, Pennsylvania.

cies...or take care of the leaky pipe under the sink!

We'd move about every third year. When we did, the sorting, packing and saying good-bye were done in a frenzy, as each preacher tried to move his family out before the next preacher arrived. At the same time, you'd try not to arrive at the new place before *that* good brother had moved.

Keep in mind that there were no U-Hauls back then; we'd use whatever was at hand—our Model T Ford or any other chariot we had, plus a borrowed truck or even the railroad as a last resort. It was always difficult to decide what to take and what to leave.

Upon arriving at our new abode, we'd often be welcomed by a "pounding". See, "pounding the preacher" was a tradition that beautifully exemplified the relationship between the church and the entire community—not just the denomination.

I believe the original idea of pounding was for each family to bring a pound of whatever it could to help augment the preacher's meager groceries. The variety never ceased to amaze us—everything from cornmeal to the most elaborately prepared sauces and desserts. Once, during the Depression, almost everyone brought a jar of blackberries. When we moved, we left 100 jars in the cellar!

Pounding was always a treat for a preacher's family—and sometimes they were literally lifesavers when our groceries had dwindled to a precarious state. What joy for a discouraged preacher's family to return home and find the kitchen tables and counters loaded down with all sorts of good food.

Thanks to the unique blessing of being brought up in country parsonages, I have a treasure chest of wonderful memories.

—*Anita Byrom*
Mesquite, Texas

Country home near Traverse City, Michigan is decked out for Christmas (top); above, St. Mary of Loreto Catholic Church outside Leland, Wisconsin. At right: historic Antelope Community Church in Wasco County in central Oregon was built in 1897.

Steve Terrill

Country church in South Woodbury, Vermont (above); at right, Bridget's Church in Cornwall Bridge, Connecticut; below, oldest general store in America, located in Bath, New Hampshire. Opposite page: rural church in East Corinth, Vermont; inset, dazzling Fourth of July fireworks.

Dick Dietrich; inset, James H. Schuey

6

J.C. Allen and Son

I was raised in a family of nine kids. For fun, my two older sisters and I used to cut paper dolls and furniture from the Sears Roebuck catalog. After cutting and cutting for hours to get the perfect family, we'd build "flat" houses on the floor, using Lincoln Logs to make the room divisions.

We also used Kleenex to make beds, although Mom was not at all happy to see us waste it for that purpose. Once in a great while, we would get a dime to buy real paper dolls, but mostly we played with the catalog variety.

Our mom still laughs today about the time one Sunday when she heard us say to each other, "I hope we don't have company today so we can play paper dolls all day long."

—*Wilma Strasburger*
Remington, Indiana

Money was scarce when I was growing up in rural South Dakota. Despite this, my parents made sure that my three sisters and I each had a doll of our own, which we truly treasured.

One particular summer, our dolls went everywhere with us. They were present as we played our days away around the farmyard and as we did our daily chores—feeding the animals, gathering eggs and caring for Dad's sick cow.

One evening, my sister Mary discovered that her doll, "Joy", was missing. We immediately searched every place we might have left her. To our disap-

pointment, we could not find Joy anywhere. Several weeks passed, and we gave up all hope of ever seeing her again. We felt as if we'd lost a very dear friend.

About this time, our hard work caring for Dad's sick cow paid off. After she recovered and returned to her herd in the pasture, we raked her bedding into a neat pile. Suddenly, Mary shrieked with excitement. There, tucked under the hay and straw, lay Joy, safe and unharmed, except for a crooked right eye.

What a sight we must have been—four girls jumping up and down with happiness, hugging Joy and each other, with tears running down our cheeks! Quite naturally, we soon found ourselves kneeling in a line along the tongue of an old hay wagon. With hands folded and heads bowed, we said a prayer of thanks to the Lord for the return of our precious Joy.

After that day, Joy was our favorite doll. Her crooked eye made her even more special. It told a tale of survival and great adventure.

—*Donna Peters, Colorado Springs, Colorado*

We grew up on a ranch that was miles away from town. We had few toys to play with, so my brother and I would use our imaginations and make play ranches in the dirt.

For fences and corrals, we'd wrap string around nails pounded into the ground. We'd use rocks for our cattle and wooden blocks for the houses and

The girl in this photo, shared by Sherron Kolb of Milpitas, California, obviously treasures her doll as much as the girls in the story at left.

barns. For horses, we'd find horned toads and tie string on their horns to guide and drive them. We spent many happy hours making these "ranches" and playing in the dirt. —*Dorothy Ferrin*
Paso Robles, California

In the early 1940's, when prosperity followed the Great Depression and we were involved in World War II, our country church began a monthly community night. It cheered us up during that somber time, and also promoted patriotism and a sense of community and friendship.

The event was held in the church basement on the first Friday of each month. We hurried to get evening chores done—livestock fed, eggs gathered and the cow milked—for we met at 8 in summer, 7:30 in winter.

Sometimes the occasion was a shower for a newlywed couple. How we enjoyed watching the handsome young folks open their gifts! Twice we welcomed a new pastor and his family. On occasion, we children watched in awe as the community embraced a young Army man who'd come home on brief furlough.

Mostly, though, it was a down-home talent show and community fellowship time. We generally sang

Many families made music together during the 1920's and '30's.

a hymn or two, then began good clean fun in which everyone could participate, from a young couple carrying their first infant to the oldest grandfather, able to get down the steps only by leaning on his cane.

Sometimes there was a musical solo or two from children taking piano or voice lessons from a teacher in our town. I remember two little girls who wore frilly matching dresses as they sang and dramatized *Playmates*. I thought for sure real tears fell when they argued over "the cellar door", but sunny smiles came when they were again "playmates".

Often there were contests, such as cow, hog and chicken calling. How we laughed at the contest between five ladies to see which of them could most successfully hammer nails into a well-dried chunk of hard, old oak tree stump. Only one was successful—a husky woman who often helped her husband on the farm.

Another time, six men were chosen to go off behind the stage curtain. They were quietly instructed to roll up their pants legs and form a line. A drape covered halfway up to their knees. Then the stage curtain was raised just high enough to expose only their hairy knees. Out in front, their wives attempted to decide which pair of knees belonged to their husband. It wasn't easy for some!

Other times, two then-unmarried brothers would sing and play violin and guitar. They'd perform popular love songs of the day, such as *Those Wedding Bells Are Breaking up That Old Gang of Mine, For Me and My Gal* and *Some Sunday Morning*.

The most rollicking fun to me as a child was the monologue given by a pleasant and plump old farm lady. She walked to the stage with a sheet of penciled notes, carrying a folding chair. Modestly she seated herself sideways to the audience and addressed us, "My dears, they've asked me to talk to you tonight, and I really don't know what to say. But I did hear a little news on the party line today."

Any adults in the audience who took jokes well might hear their names mentioned in outrageously—and extremely unlikely—gossipy stories. She poked gentle fun in every way possible, most of all at her small meek husband. Her famous line was, "My sakes, dears, you'll never guess what happened next!"

We were always sorry when the program ended, but there were "the eats" to console us. Refreshments were planned ahead, with each family bringing pies and sandwiches, or cookies and fruit salad, or—best of all—homemade ice cream with cake.

The committee to plan the next community night was announced before we all left for home, and their phones were busy first thing Saturday morning, lining up events for the next performance.
—*Elaine Carr, Nyssa, Oregon*

Living on a farm was hard, but it was also fun. We were rather poor and, as a result, we didn't have store-bought toys. Instead, we created our own or invented things to do.

For instance, old sardine cans made great pretend boats to float in the canal. We used them for cars, wagons and various other things.

We made little roads in the hollow just to the side of our garden, where we also dug small caves and canyon roads. It was quite a wonderful place to play.

We made model wagons as well. Once my brother found some small metal wheels and made a really great one. It didn't wear out or get broken like our wooden ones. And since wagons called for a pioneer trail, we proceeded to make a long road for our small wagons. It ran up through the cedars and through some of the draws.

I remember one day when my brother and I were laying out a "campsite" for the wagons. We were kneeling on the ground arranging moss, when all of a sudden our dog, "Tobe", chased a rabbit toward us. It ran right into my brother and knocked itself out. My brother then hit it with a stick and we had rabbit for supper that night.
—*Eugene Barker*
American Fork, Utah

With a little imagination, farm children didn't need toys to amuse themselves.

We grew up with a creek and a blackberry patch to entertain us in the summertime, along with a big old cypress hedge behind the house where we played "Tarzan" and had playhouses and hideouts. In winter, the barn was our playground; we'd do acrobatics with the hay fork rope and put on plays .

I was "Dad's girl" and, as such, had my own string of gentle, easy-to-milk cows. We sang in time to the rhythm of the milk pail, told jokes, laughed and squirted milk into the cat's mouth. To me, the cow barn was a friendly, fun place.

I could write a whole book of farm memories, but I'm still too busy living it up in this small community where we're woven so much into the fabric of life. —*Dorothy Halliday, Point Arena, California*

Making ice cream in winter was a real treat. We used the ice that formed in a big barrel that caught rainwater from a gutter pipe. We'd fill a dish with ice cream and eat it in front of a fire—delicious!

Also in winter, my stepfather's five nephews, who were natural-born musicians, would go around and play at peoples' houses once every 2 or 3 weeks. They played the violin, guitar, mandolin, bass fiddle and harmonica and were the best band I ever heard.

About once a month, there'd be a play party at someone's house. There we'd sing songs and dance. One family had an outdoor dance floor and often held ice cream suppers and square dances at their home. It was lots of good clean entertainment. —*Lillian Edge*
Owensboro, Kentucky

Good-natured practical jokes entertained rural folks and harmlessly occupied their children. My 87-year-old dad attests to fun in the early days with his tales of overturned outhouses, an accidentally broken school flagpole, and tiny Christmas gifts hidden in folds of tissue paper deep within large brightly wrapped packages.

Grandpa Bothamley (Dad's father) and his long-standing friend, a neighboring

farmer, tried to outwit each other every year by hiding their melon patches. It seems the neighbor always managed to swipe a ripe melon from Grandpa's patch.

One year, Grandpa knew he'd outwitted his friend at last. He planted his melons in the middle of a cornfield! The large patch was nicely concealed by the growing corn. Then one day, Grandpa was spring-toothing nearby when he spied his neighbor's little brown-and-white spotted dog running into the cornfield. "That man's checking out my melons," thought Grandpa. "I'll catch him in the act."

Grandpa tied his horses to a fence post, but when he reached the melons, no one was there. The joke was on Grandpa, because when he got back to his work, the horses were busily going up and down the field with Grandpa's neighbor in charge.

Of course, as Dad recalls, Grandpa still invited the neighbor, his family and others for cold watermelon on Friday nights. He always planted extra for whatever mischief and fun might occur.

—*Janice Girton, Sturgis, Michigan*

Farm life was hard for families when I was growing up in the 1940's, but we had our fun times, too. My brother made us walking stilts, or would put a box on our wagon and make a pretend car that "pulled" us around the farm.

We built tree houses—and got in trouble for using Dad's good nails! In winter, Dad and my brother would cut blocks of ice from the creek and make ice cream, which we'd enjoy eating in front of the fire.

Corncob mountain provides perfect place to play "king of the hill".

I remember one year when the snow was deep, my sister and brother started rolling a snowball at the top of the hill by our house. By the time they got it to the back gate, it was 4 or 5 feet high! They left it there when they came inside to warm up. It froze to the ground and Dad had to help them move it. —*Shirley Duckett, Piedmont, Missouri*

The barn was my favorite place to play at my grandparents' farm. I loved the smell of hay and cows and horses. When the hay supply was low and before the new hay was put into the barn, the haymow was mostly empty.

This left plenty of room for fun. We'd hang a bag swing—a gunnysack stuffed with hay or straw—from a long rope attached to the rafters. We'd stand on a huge mound of hay at the far end of the room and someone would swing the bag up to us until we grabbed it.

We'd jump on by straddling the bag. And while holding on to the rope, we'd swoop clear across the barn and back again. That was the ultimate in fun! —*Pat Leek, Laporte, Minnesota*

For fun on the farm, we made playhouses by outlining "rooms" with rows of stones, leaving gaps for doorways. In the "kitchen", we'd make a stove out of four bricks, using boards for its shelves.

The bundle wagon also served as a playhouse, as did the corncrib—after the corn was shelled. The short boards that filled the track for the corn sheller drags were just right for the stove shelves. Our junk barrel provided lots of fun, too—pretty pieces of glass or crockery, which we handled carefully, served as plates. Salmon cans were highly prized because they made excellent mud pie pans.

This was our recipe for mud pies: one salmon can three-fourths full of fine dirt; one handful of cement taken from the bag in the crib driveway; one or two eggs; and enough water to make a stiff "batter".

We'd stir the mixture with a twig and carefully pour it into a "pan", then bake it for several days in the brick oven or in the sun. This would make quite a durable mud pie. In fact, they lasted a bit too long, which aroused Dad's suspicions. He found out about the cement, which earned us a trip across his knee!

We played store with selected tin cans, bottles and jars that still had decent-looking labels. We also built parks, using weed blossoms for flowers and tall weeds for trees. Paths led through our parks to goldfish ponds, which really were salmon cans sunk into the ground.

On hot days, we'd swim in the livestock tank or ride the swing in the pear tree near the shop. There was only one swing, which caused problems—until Daddy made us a lovely swing set out of brace posts. —*Frances Weiss, Oswego, Illinois*

I can still remember the day I decided to play sailor on the Shiocton River, which bordered our farm and overflowed each spring, flooding a nearby marsh.

I was 8 years old on that cold and windy day when I took my mother's washtub and a board for

Swings like this one are dear to the hearts of country kids.

a paddle and headed for the marsh. I was having some fun on that vast span of water when suddenly, my tub got hung up on something.

My efforts to free the tub tipped it over. Fortunately, the water wasn't very deep, though I did get a cold, cold dunking. I walked slowly to shore and headed for the house, wondering what my folks would think when they saw me wet and cold.

Dad was the first to show sympathy. He used a couple whacks from his huge hand to warm up the part of my body used for sitting. At that precise moment, I decided I didn't want to be a sailor anymore.

—*Arthur Laehn, Clintonville, Wisconsin*

Competitions like this 1935 National Corn Husking Contest in Newtown, Indiana grabbed the attention of rural residents.

I'll never forget the Saturday night in October 1935 when we anxiously waited to see if one of our neighbors, Hobart Ray, had won the state corn husking contest. I was only 11 years old, but I can still recall the tension of the evening.

There were great expectations, since Hobart had placed third in the contest a year earlier. Hobart, his wife, Bessie, and their children lived about a quarter of a mile from us.

He farmed 180 acres, mostly corn, and had developed quite a reputation as an outstanding corn husker, or shucker.

There were no mechanical corn pickers in those days. To pick corn, a man needed a shucking hook, which fit over a glove and allowed him to rip an ear of corn from the stalk, then rake the ear clean of dried husks before tossing it against a high sideboard on a wagon, also known as the "bang board" for obvious reasons.

As I recall, a good man could shuck 100 bushels of corn in a day, provided the conditions were right. That meant every ear of corn in each bushel had to be jerked free from the stalk, husks pulled away clean and stripped from each ear, and the ear tossed into the wagon.

We were all gathered that night to listen to radio station KFEQ out of St. Joseph, Missouri, which was going to announce the results. There were more visitors at our home than normal, probably because we had one of the only radios in the area.

Generous supplies of popcorn and apples were in evidence, and the *Grand Ole Opry* blared from the radio. Every chair was occupied by an adult, and kids were sprawled here and there in this or another room, some asleep and others feasting on the popcorn and apples. The tension mounted and mounted. Surely this was Hobart's year!

And we weren't only excited about possibly hearing Hobart named champion. We were also expecting to hear the name of someone we knew on the radio, which was a big thing back then. Even more, he'd receive a grandiose prize of $50 for winning the contest—big bucks in the depths of the drought and Depression.

Suddenly everyone grew quiet as the time for the announcement drew nigh. Then, doom struck

J.C. Allen and Son

with the suddenness of a lightning bolt. Someone other than Hobart had won. It was a cruel fate to an 11-year-old boy whose heart was set on knowing a local champion. It was only small consolation when the announcer told us Hobart had finished third, earning $15 in prize money.

Sometime around midnight, Hobart himself arrived at our house, having hitchhiked from the contest. He seemed happy enough. After a round of greetings and congratulations, our visitors began to head for home, some on horseback, some in Model T Fords or whatever.

Over the years, I've realized what a tremendous feat it was for Hobart to win third place in the contest 2 years in a row. Countless good men were desperate in those days for any amount of money, so the contest was no mere game. No doubt the champion was as hardworking and honorable as our local favorite. But he had, after all, beaten our hero, and that was hard to take.
—*Thomas Brown*
Trenton, Missouri

As a kid on the farm during the Great Depression, my favorite recreation was fishing. We usually fished by setting trot lines, which consisted of a long line strung over the creek between two trees and shorter lines with baited hooks that were tied to the main line and hung in the water.

We'd run the lines early in the evening. By next morning, it was not unusual to have six or eight catfish, one on each hook. We'd then have catfish for breakfast, a special treat for all of us.

I loved Sundays in the summer. After chores, we might do some fishing, but in the evenings, we often made ice cream. We had our own milk and eggs —all we needed was a chunk of ice, which required just a dime and a horseback ride to the local store. There was only one flavor of ice cream, and that was vanilla; we'd never heard of any other flavor.

Our other entertainment revolved around the theater in town, 12 miles away. Each Christmas and on birthdays, the theater would give each schoolchild a free pass and a bag of candy. Most of the time, we'd walk the 12 miles for that treat. That was a real fun time.

After the one who went to the movie got home, the rest of the family would gather around the living room and listen to everything the moviegoer saw and heard. They usually never left out one detail.
—*Alvin Mast, Chico, California*

Fishing was a favorite form of recreation for many country kids.

The big bonus for children during threshing time was the opportunity to go to town on Friday evenings and/or Sunday afternoons to watch softball games. Our dads and brothers became pitchers, catchers or fielders on a threshing-ring softball team, as the Giertzes played the Gierkes and the Nordmeyers and other threshing-ring teams.

They played just as hard as they worked, but with one difference—this was fun! Women and children watched from the few bleacher seats and cheered. If there were refreshments available, they were unimportant—we couldn't afford them anyway.

The fun lay in the atmosphere of relaxation and association with friends and relatives without responsibilities involved. It was pure pleasure.

I remember those years of long ago, before the invention of the combine eliminated shocking oats and threshing tasks. I remember the hot, dusty work and the happy, exciting threshing-ring softball games.   —*Viola Brault, Chebanse, Illinois*

I was raised in isolated farming country in the late 1940's, before there were road improvements. We had the usual community centers of school, church and general store.

But the one real plus was a big creek that flowed through the area, originating in the mountains some 10 miles distant. The creek abounded with fish and scattered deeper pools, suitable for skinny dipping. A larger one, about 100 yards long and ankle to 8 feet deep, provided family fun.

From mid-May until Labor Day, as farm chores permitted, people of all ages would be there, splashing and swimming or diving from rocks at the deep end.

Playing in the creek seated in me a lifelong love of water. Since I've grown up and moved around, I've always availed myself of swimming op-

Nothing beat the heat on a hot summer day like a dip in the local swimming hole.

portunities. However, no pool has ever matched the hole in the creek near my childhood home.
—*Auton Miller, Piney Flats, Tennessee*

For fun on the farm, the boys loved to get on 100-gallon barrels and try to ride them across the yard. Needless to say, there were many spills.

We also played "snip and snap", a game where we pasted six of the same items on six cards, and six of another item on another set of six cards and so on. Then we would turn them over in a pile and take turns flipping the cards to see if they matched. If you didn't get a match, you put them in the "snip" pile in the middle of the table. It was fun; I even made these cards for my four boys.

We played "marbles" with acorn nuts, especially during Christmas, when they were plentiful and chewy. We also made chains by hooking together weeds that looked like four-leaf clovers.
—*Lilly Klos, Baker, Montana*

Growing up in the 1920's and '30's, we often made our own entertainment by means of imagination and invention. My sisters and I sometimes made stilts to walk on and even fixed a stick to roll a hoop.

Another of our fun toys was the can and string for telephones. After we'd set up housekeeping—perhaps one home by the lilacs and another under an elm tree across the yard—we would call our "neighbor" on the can phones.

It was also fun making ballet dancers out of hollyhock flowers. We would line them up on boxes and pretend we had a store full of ballerina dolls for sale. Sometimes our store would sell soda fizzes, made with vinegar, baking soda and water. They were fun to make, but not too good to drink. We loved mixing them to see the fizz—until Mom put a stop to wasting her soda and vinegar!

Another of our joys was going downtown on Saturday nights. All the farmers and families would come to purchase groceries and supplies for the following week. It was fun to meet friends and attend band concerts on the courthouse lawn. I loved being there when the band was setting up in the bandstand and listening as they tuned their instruments.

Our Depression toys and entertainment provided us with lots of pleasure. We were happy children and didn't realize what we didn't have, for most of our friends lived in much the same manner.

—*Irene Dunn, Hope, Idaho*

In summer, when it was hot and dry, Mama and Daddy would be busy with fieldwork on our beautiful Wisconsin farm. That's when Mama would tell me to take my sister and go and play.

One of those times, when I was about 10 years old, I had a bright idea. I told Joan that we'd start our own museum. It would be such a good museum that movie stars and governors—maybe even the President—would come to see it.

We ran to an old empty corncrib on wheels that sat out in back of our barn. "This should be just perfect," I said. "We could clean this up really good. Then we could take the boards Daddy stacked up in front of the door and use them for shelves." We got busy and cleaned the corncrib but good.

After that, we went up the creek and to the woods to hunt for museum items. We found a lot of things to make the best nature museum in the whole world—from the creek, pretty colored stones of all shapes and sizes, a dried-up crab claw and lively tadpoles; from the woods, an abandoned bird's nest, pieces of beautiful bird eggshells and blue jay and goldfinch feathers.

We found an old rooster's tail feather, and put many insects—caterpillars, angleworms, lightning bugs, grasshoppers, potato bugs and others—in glass jars. We also displayed many kinds of leaves, unusual pieces of wood, tree bark and fuzzy green moss that we found on rocks.

We were sure the President would come to see our museum, though he never did. This is one of the ways we found to entertain ourselves out in the country, where there were no neighbor children to play with. We used our imaginations because we did not have very many games or toys. —*Carol Myers Reedsburg, Wisconsin*

When I was a teenager, church lawn parties were big events, and we spent weeks discussing one while it was in the making. They were held at someone's house under a makeshift shelter with a counter all around where folks were served food and drink.

The menu never varied—hot dogs, homemade ice

Big straw hat helps this little lady keep her cool—and have some fun.

cream and all kinds of homemade pies and cakes. The food, especially the homemade ice cream, was great. But for the teenagers, the games were the big event.

Our favorite was "tap hands". All the boys and girls formed a circle and held hands. If you were "it", you'd walk around the circle until you reached the person you were sweet on. You'd gently tap the person's hand, join hands and walk around the cir-

J.C. Allen and Son

Farm communities eagerly anticipated picnic dinners like this one on the banks of the Tippecanoe River near Winamac, Indiana in 1928.

cle, then drop the person back off in their place. Then it was their turn to repeat the whole thing.

I can still remember after all these years how I longed to be picked by my favorite beau, and how thrilled I was when he chose me.

Many times the lawn parties climaxed with a box social. The girls packed a large supper in a beautifully decorated box that was sold to the highest bidder. No one was supposed to know whose box they were bidding for, but the news usually leaked out. The one who bought the box ate with the one who prepared it.

Those were truly the good old days. —*Ruby Neese*
Liberty, North Carolina

My great-grandparents raised me, but they both passed away when I was 13, so I went to live with a couple who had adopted one of my brothers. They were also a farm family.

My foster father was full of devilment. You nev-

er knew what he was going to do. I can remember one week in particular when everything had gone well on the farm for all of us, so he was especially full of pranks. My foster mother and I kept telling him we'd get even.

One day we had a heavy rain in the afternoon and evening, so the next day it was too wet to get into the fields. Father thought this would be a good time to do preventive maintenance on the farm equipment.

When Mother and I saw him lying under the combine to do some greasing, she said, "Come, Peggy. Now's our chance!" We each got a 5-gallon bucket of water and threw it on him at the same time. We dropped the buckets and ran as fast as we could to the house.

We were busy fixing dinner and giggling when all of a sudden Father came in the back door with the water hose and drenched both of us, the kitchen and dinner. By the time Mother and I got finished cleaning up the water, we decided Father had "one-upped" us again.

—*Peggy Smith McIwain*
Iron City, Georgia

Today you hop in your automobile and drive 2 or 3 blocks, maybe 5 or 10 miles, maybe 50 or 100 miles. This may take 2 minutes of pre-planning, and off you go.

Not so in the early 1930's. We utilized horses and, in winter, sleighs. That was all we had for transportation, particularly when the roads were blocked with snow.

Our family had some close friends—not miles

close, but friendship close—who we enjoyed visiting. They lived about 10 miles away by road, but 3 miles or so by horse and sleigh. The roads running to their home were blocked for about 4 months every winter.

They lived so far back on small country roads that the snowplowers never knew a road existed, let alone that a family lived way back there. But we knew. So, about once a month, we planned a visit to their home, and in between, they visited us. We didn't have to call ahead to see if they would be home—we knew they'd always be there.

Preparing for the visit was like getting ready for a week-long vacation to Mexico, though not as warm. We put our flat stones on the stove to warm up—an all-day task. Then we filled the sleigh with hay about 3 to 4 feet deep. At about 5 o'clock, we'd harness our two favorite sleigh horses, putting four or five long strings of tinkling bells on their harnesses.

We'd do our chores, eat an early dinner and depart from home about 6, our way lit by lanterns hung from the front of the sleigh. Usually we'd pick up a neighbor family along the way—another four or six people.

We had loads of fun going across fields and over two lakes to our destination. After the first mile, we'd usually toss someone out of the sleigh or jump out and play tag. We loved the trip over.

When we got to our friends' house, we'd unhitch the horses, put them in their barn, and feed and blanket them. Then we'd have the entire remaining evening for fun.

The parents would play cards from about 8 to midnight. The young folks would head outdoors and skate on Eagle Lake, ski, slide down the hills on sleds or skis, or play in the hay barn. We'd never bother our parents for that 4 hours—we'd be having too much fun!

"Lunch" was always served about 12:30 a.m. Not just a small snack, mind you, but a good hearty farmer's meal. About 1:30 a.m., we'd hitch up our horses and have another grand time returning home by moonlight, running along beside the sleigh, singing and enjoying every minute of the way.

No one ever complained about getting cold—and I'm certain it was just as cold in 1930 as it is today.

—Curtis Nelson, Eagan, Minnesota

Sleigh rides provided plenty of winter fun—and sometimes were the only means of winter transportation!

I grew up on a farm in a very close-knit community. Seven families of my relatives lived in this area. During the Depression and 3 drought years, we had a tough time, but everyone helped each other.

Our community attended a one-room church and school, and lots of our recreation involved attending ice cream socials, political rallies and memorial services. We often walked to Sunday school and church, and attended soup and pie suppers and literary meetings with skits, jokes and singing. There were birthday parties held each month, and women took cakes and made coffee, tea and lemonade.

During summer, we often had ice cream parties and family reunions—everyone would get together for a big meal and yard games like "drop the handkerchief", "kick the can", "May I?" and charades. We

133

held country picnics, swam in creeks and roasted wieners and marshmallows. We went to church on Sundays, followed by rousing ball games in the afternoon and hymn singing in the evening.

In fall, we had taffy pulls and Halloween parties. The whole family dressed up in homemade outfits—no store-bought costumes or masks back then. We wore brown and black cotton stockings pulled over our heads for masks, with eyes and mouths cut out.

In winter, we rode sleds pulled by a faithful old horse, built snow forts, had snowball fights, skated on the ponds, rode horses or walked to parties at neighbors' houses. My uncle taught us games. We played checkers and dominoes and square-danced.

J.C. Allen and Son

An unusual swing provided hours of fun for these children.

Every Christmas, a program was held at our one-room school, and kids received oranges, apples and candy. I met my future husband at such a Christmas program.

When young folks reached dating age, families only had one vehicle—either a car or truck—so we often rode horses to attend various events in our community.

If a girl had a date with a boy who could borrow his father's vehicle and if he had $1, you could go to town and see a double feature for 25¢ each. Then you could go to a restaurant and get two hamburgers for 25¢, two Cokes at 10¢ each and with the nickel left, buy a package of Wrigley's gum. That was considered a fantastic date.

We never felt poor or deprived and were never bored. It was a wonderful time to grow up.

—*Pauline Longnecker, West Plains, Missouri*

Who can ever forget the old front veranda! It served many a purpose—a place to hold tea parties for imaginary guests and a quiet spot to read a book or, in later years, to sit and play the accordion.

You could always find a shady nook on it on a hot summer's day. But one great thing was the dry soft soil underneath it that turned into the greatest mud pies and alphabet letters, much to our mother's chagrin. My brother, Ricky, played with his cars and tractors under there, building hills and ditches and roadways.

Even our old dog, "Dandy", loved the cool recesses under the veranda, and pet lambs were often found using it for a sleeping spot.   —*Elma Kozuk*
Riverton, Manitoba

After the threshing or silo-filling seasons were over, there was usually an ice cream party at one of the neighboring homes. This was a very fun time in the community as the families gathered for social time after a lot of hard work.

There were other fun times, too. We had a long summer kitchen and were often hosts to square dances. At the beginning of the evening, the men would carry all the furniture outdoors. We'd sprinkle cornmeal over the wood floor to slicken it so feet could glide more easily. Neighbors and friends from the community would arrive and some would bring other friends along.

Someone who could play a violin, guitar or concertina would provide music, and another would call the squares. We had room for as many as three squares. Occasionally my uncle and his sons would come with their fiddle and guitars to provide music.

At the close of the evening, carry-in refreshments would be served and the men would return the furniture to its place. It was a fun time in those Depression days of the 1930's.   —*Dorothy Stephenson Hanna, Indiana*

Formal entertainment was hard to come by in an era of hard times. The Great Depression had deprived most people of the means to travel to the cities, and even if they were able to do so, there was little to do once they arrived, for it was far too expensive.

Therefore, our entertainment came in the form of house parties. One or another member of the community would set aside a day for a party and advertising was done by word of mouth. On the appointed date, everyone gathered at dusk for an evening of fun and games with their neighbors.

The women would bring their knitting or simply share recipes, and the men talked crops, hard times or wondered just who would be the winner in the upcoming election.

But the night belonged to the young. The youngest of the children claimed the yard as their turf, and squeals of delight prevailed as they marched around the house, playing "ain't no boogers out tonight" or bouncing a ball on someone's tin roof.

The little-used living room was set aside as the exclusive territory for the teenagers. That awkward period between being a child and not quite an adult was a cause of consternation for some, while others saw it as their chance for a 5-minute "date" with a member of the opposite sex they'd been too shy to approach before.

At precisely 11 p.m., the father of the house would announce bedtime, and the parents would gather the now-sleeping children and carry them home, with the reluctant teenagers following, still dreaming of that wonderful 5-minute date with so-and-so.

Good, wholesome entertainment of our own making provided a distraction from the hard work required by hard times, and at the same time was instrumental in forming lasting friendships—even marriages.

House parties like this one offered neighbors a chance to relax and socialize during the Depression.

How many young people today could comprehend a date where there was no movie, dinner and dancing, or even a long drive in a convertible?
—*John Sellers, Sunset Beach, North Carolina*

Homemade toys are "Deere" to these boys; inset, unusual sledding technique.

Hitching a ride back home (above); continuing clockwise: tire swing is a time-honored country favorite; swimming hole is a perfect place to cool off; boy's out on a limb with tree house.

137

Quiet moment in the barn (above); continuing clockwise: testing the produce; budding architects build sand castle; practice makes perfect as boy shoots for all the marbles.

You can almost hear the sleigh bells in photo at right; continuing clockwise: waiting for a bite at the fishing hole; boy whiles away the hours on Pennsylvania creek; young lady daydreams on a haystack.

7

J.C. Allen and Son

Farm Families

My parents were living on a small farm in northwestern Missouri when I was born in 1937. Times were hard, and they were already having a difficult time paying for their farm and taking care of their little family—my brother and sister.

Before I was born, they wondered how they would ever pay the medical bill for my birth. But during the winter, my dad figured things out. He decided to raise a large patch of cucumbers and sell them to a pickle factory located just over the state line in Iowa.

Dad had a great crop that year. I was born the last of August, and he was able to pay the medical bills with money from the cucumbers. As a result, Dad had a pet name that he called me for years—his little "pickle puss".

—*Marjorie Traxler, Exline, Iowa*

Marjorie Traxler, 4, with cat "Puff". Her dad nicknamed her "little pickle puss"

Almost all of the education I've ever needed in life came from my father while I was growing up in the late 1940's on a small farm in East Texas.

My father, whom my four brothers and sisters and I affectionately called Papa, was the greatest teacher in the whole world. He taught us about love when he danced with us in the sparsely decorated living room that also served as my parents' bedroom.

Depending on our size, he would hold us in his arms, let us stand on his shoes or take our hands and waltz across the linoleum floor to the music of Bob Wills and The Texas Playboys. At other times, he'd play his fiddle as we danced with Mama, instilling a love in us that would last a lifetime.

Papa taught us joy because he always whistled when he worked. No matter how hard the task, how hot the summer or how little money we had, you could hear him whistling any number of tunes—or some he just made up as he went along. To this day, it brings me great joy to hear myself whistling Papa's tunes, no matter how difficult the going may be at the time.

On many occasions, Papa proved he was indeed a man of peace. Once when money was shorter than a duck's tail, we took a lamb to auction to get a little cash. While Papa was registering our lamb in the auction barn office, two less-than-honest men approached my brother and me and asked, "Do you want to sell that fine lamb for $1?"

We readily agreed, thinking how proud Papa would be. When Papa returned, we happily gave him the dollar. No doubt the lamb would have sold for a great deal more, and the money was badly needed. But Papa just said, "That's great! Now we don't have to waste time trying to sell that crit-

ter. Time is money, you know."

He wouldn't have thought about pursuing those two culprits, figuring they probably needed the money worse than we did.

Goodness was evident in everything Papa did. He always helped out neighbors without asking for anything in return. Once he lowered me down a neighbor's well on a draw bucket to fish out a dead raccoon. The smell was terrible, so Papa put a clothespin on my nose.

I held onto the bucket with one hand and netted the drowned raccoon with the other. The neighbor lady wanted to pay me, but Papa said, "That's not necessary. It was a good experience for him— something to tell his grandchildren about." At the time, I didn't agree with him, but now it's one of my all-time favorite stories.

Papa also displayed goodness by helping Mama wash clothes every Saturday morning, using the wringer washer we had on the back porch, drawing water from the well and hanging clothes on the line. He helped her with cooking and canning, too. As Mama said, "A man like Papa was hard to find."

Building our sense of responsibility, pride and confidence was Papa's specialty. For instance, he'd mail us packets of cotton or tomato seeds in special envelopes with a letter he had made up from the "Department of Agriculture". It would ask us to plant and take care of the "experimental" seeds.

The letter would close by saying, "We have complete faith in your ability to help with this project. Please send us your results." With this official approach, Papa would help us grow our little test plots.

I'll be forever grateful that I was raised on a farm—and happier still that Papa was there to raise us and teach us through his example. You see, Papa married my mother and took in my two older brothers and me when I was just 3 years old. Later, my younger brother and sister were born, and not once in our lives can I remember Papa showing any favoritism to his biological children. My last name may be different than Papa's, but the heart is the same.   —*Terry Curtis, Austin, Texas*

During the Depression, my parents were lucky enough to buy a very poor 84-acre farm in Lebanon County, Pennsylvania for $2,800. It had a large farmhouse, a barn and four other buildings. I

Hard work and pride helped Curtis Darkes (tallest boy) and his large family, shown here in 1937, revive a neglected farm in Pennsylvania.

call it a poor farm because the soil was rocky and full of rain gullies and swampy areas with clay soil. The meadow was overgrown with briar thickets and weeds.

We moved our possessions from a rented house

by making several 2-mile trips with a hay wagon drawn by two mules. The last 1/4-mile down our lane, off the main dirt road, was axle-deep in mud.

This was the beginning of a new life for our parents and us children—10 in all. In time, five more children followed. The kids who were 6 or older were kept busy with chores from early morning until late at night, 6 days a week. On Sundays, we went to church, and work was limited to caring for livestock and preparing meals.

Perseverance, necessity and determination to "make a farm out of this place" paid off after years of back-breaking labor. We removed tons of rocks of all sizes and used them to pave our lane. We filled the gullies with whatever didn't cost money.

We spread all the manure we could acquire and, after a time, could buy lime for one field per year. Eventually, we increased our crop yield to the point where we could proudly call our place a *real* farm.

Our parents' character and determination pulled us through. I'm very proud to have been part of a farm family in that era. It was a hard life, but I know none of us have any regrets. It taught us to appreciate contentment, which frequently comes when you've done your best. I know—I was there!

—*Curtis Darkes, Hamilton, New Jersey*

Some of my earliest memories are of a winter-time when my mom's parents had to move and couldn't find a place to live. So they came to our house for the winter.

We had a huge living room that we used to shut off for the winter, as we only had a big wood stove in the dining room and, of course, a wood range in the kitchen. So Grandma and Grandpa moved into the living room.

The one thing I really remember is that Grandpa always took an Alka-Seltzer before bedtime, and the four of us girls used to fight over who got to drop the tablet in the water and watch it fizz. How's that for a crazy memory!

When my two oldest sisters were big enough, Dad claimed them as his helpers. My next oldest sister was Mom's main helper. As the baby of the family, I just brought the cows in from the pasture and fetched things from our garden, which supplied most of our food.

Then we had a new addition—a brother who took my place as the "baby". I loved him so much it never occurred to me that he was taking my niche in the family; instead, I became his keeper. He was also my playmate, and we used to play house or try to ride the pigs out in the hog lot.

We had a wonderful childhood, being blessed with parents who taught us how important it was to be honest and that any job worth doing is worth doing right.

—*Mrs. Robert Johnston*
Dodge Center, Minnesota

Cooperation among family members was critical to completing important tasks like harvesting.

I was born and raised during the Depression on my grandparents' farm in southern Wisconsin. It

143

was a large farm, so my younger sister and I, along with two cousins who lived on a neighboring farm, had the run of miles of countryside.

We had many adventures that brought us great pleasure in remembering through the years. How wonderful to have had those endless summer days to plan adventures and experience the freedom of farm life! —*Pauline Olson, Albany, Wisconsin*

My grandmother was a never-ending source of creativity, with volumes of ingenious ideas about how to amuse my brother and me. One of the best games she invented was based on her recollections of traveling in a stagecoach with her parents and little brother over the Western prairies in the mid-1800's, bouncing about as the wheels sank into the prairie dog tunnels.

At her house, "Stagecoach" was a parlor game, literally, as there were six matched side chairs there and a very long settee. We'd set the chairs in twos, side by side, and pretend they were our team of horses. Placing the team at one end of the sofa, our stagecoach, we'd draw a rope through small notches in the chair backs. This arrangement served as our reins.

With a shout to our team to "Giddyap!", we'd take the reins, jump onto the coach and race up the trail, allowing our fertile imaginations to run wild in our scenarios of the Old West. To further intrigue us, our grandmother would set up part of the room like a stopover of the times. Bellowing in unison a hearty "Whoa!" to the weary horses, we'd alight from the coach, tired, hungry and thirsty af-

ter a long day of traveling the dusty trail.

The fare offered to us at the "inn" was usually cool milk and homemade cookies. There we'd rest for the night, our heads on soft sofa cushions. At "daybreak", we'd continue our journey across the prairie, remaining ever alert for prairie dog holes, rattlesnakes and unfriendly Indians.

More than 50 years later, my brother and I recall with sweet nostalgia our childhood fantasies with a dear and remarkable grandmother. —*Mary Stark Dalmatia, Pennsylvania*

The earliest memories I have of my dad involve sitting on his lap to put my shoes on early in the morning while Mama cooked breakfast. As soon as breakfast was over, he'd go off to the fields for the day, so we wouldn't see him again until supper.

My mother was very busy with gardening, cooking and sewing, but she was always talking, laughing or singing. We teased her because she even talked to herself.

She was a wonderful cook and could make a feast from black-eyed peas, corn bread and sweet potatoes— all staples from our garden.

But I think my fondest memories of Mama are of her holding me on a rocking

Mary Parsons (in front) with her dad and sister Lucy on "Old Sunday" in 1928.

chair in front of the fireplace and reading or reciting nursery rhymes or singing funny songs until I'd fall asleep.

The fireplace was the center of our winter evenings. It was our only source of heat except the kitchen stove, and if the weather was very cold, we sat close enough that sometimes we got red splotches on our legs. We'd heat "smoothing irons", which kept our feet warm in bed. We'd wrap them in towels to keep from getting burned.

My sister, Lucy, was very special to me. She was 8 years older than me, so she was more like a second mother than a sister, except that she was so tiny that I soon caught up with her in size. She allowed me and my friends to play dress-up in her petite dresses when she was a teenager.

She helped me cut out paper dolls from mail-order catalogs and taught me how to sew and embroider. As I learned to read, she brought books for me from the school library. She actually taught me to read before I started school, just by making it such a pleasant daily activity.

—*Mary Parsons, Lometa, Texas*

We were raised in a small town known as Skyland, located in the western mountains of North Carolina. The community we grew up in was known as Pinners Cove, which was founded by my grandmother, Rozella Pinner Hare.

The community was close-knit. Grandfather Hare was the preacher at the local Baptist church, and Grandfather Anderson was the singing leader. My father and mother, Andrew and Frances Hare, were married at a very young age. I have three brothers older than me and a brother 8 years younger.

We lived on a 55-acre farm in a two-room log cabin. My dad had a Works Progress Administration job. I always thought that was something really important; little did I know that, at the time, we were just getting by!

My mom, who is now 83, was always the one who kept the farm going. She and the three older boys planted the crops. She was good with a horse-drawn plow; in fact, she could harness the horse and plow much better than my dad could!

Taking care of my baby brother while my mom and brothers worked in the fields was my main job. I'd carry him to the fields so my mother could nurse him. After he was fed, I'd take him back to the house for his nap. When he'd awaken, I'd play with him, pretending he was my baby doll.

I also cooked the noon-day meal. I can still smell, taste and see the fresh potatoes, peas, wilted lettuce, onions and corn bread. We always kept buttermilk in the spring box until it was time to eat. One of my brothers and I used to churn the milk, often arguing about who was working the hardest to make it turn into butter.

Along with all the work we did, we also had fun. My mother was a very humorous person. I recall that when some of my brothers and I would have to go to the spring af-

This mother, like one in story at left, played an important role in keeping the farm running smoothly.

ter dark to get water for the night and the next morning, she'd always get one that was left behind to wear a sheet and scare them. And while that one scared the others, *she* would wear a sheet and go around the house to scare the whole group! This happened quite often, night after night!

Now I'm 62 and a widow for 2 years. I count my blessings for growing up poor and living on a farm. It would be delightful to go back to that same time and place. Life was hard then, but I just thought that was life!
—*Marian Hare Riddle*
Fletcher, North Carolina

Making music together like the family in this photo provided many happy memories for Fay Brown Brickey.

Growing up in a big farm family—six brothers and two sisters—in the 1940's with dirt roads and no electricity, indoor plumbing, school buses or heated cars was truly the best experience anyone could ask for. Why? Because we all had to work together to accomplish anything!

Take the muddy dirt roads, for instance. I can't even remember them stopping us. We just simply gunned the car for all it was worth, and if we got stuck, we all got out and pushed, whether we were dressed up or not.

I'll forever remember Daddy, always in bib over-alls, coming into the house to get a drink of water from the bucket after being outside plowing with the horses or cutting wood. I remember him sharpening sticks so we could help strip the cane to make sorghum.

Another thing we grew up with was music! My twin sisters and I started playing guitar and mandolin at the age of 12, learning from two of our older brothers. Mother played the French harp. We played together many times and always ended the night playing and singing.

One night my parents moved everything out of two rooms to hold a square dance for friends and neighbors. Mother made sandwiches, coffee and a big kettle of hot cocoa. Ah, the wonderful sounds of laughter as we played and danced the night away.

As I fondly recall these memories, it was working together, the art of conversation and good down-home music that glued us country people together. And that's what it was like growing up in a farm family.
—*Fay Brown Brickey*
Lone Jack, Missouri

The woman I'm writing about is not a famous one. Her name won't be found in a history book or any other writing, and the only headline she ever made was her obituary in the newspaper. But she, like so many others like her, helped make Oklahoma what it is today.

She came to Indian Territory in 1904 from Tennessee. She was a young widow with two very small sons, and was accompanied by her parents and 10 brothers and sisters and their families.

They settled in a small farming community in the south part of Pontotoc County.

Being the oldest child in this large family, she'd had to help raise the other children, so she knew what hard work was all about. She helped in the fields, tended to the sick, scrubbed clothes on a rub board, dressed hogs and basically did any job she could get to support her sons and herself. She gave what money she could to her parents.

In 1908, she remarried and she, her husband and her sons moved to a farm. Their home was a dugout, a type of house that was prevalent in the early 1900's. As their family grew to include four little girls, they started to build a home and a community.

Neither she nor her husband had more than a sixth-grade education. She went through the sixth grade three times—not because she couldn't learn, but because that was as high as the grades went and she wanted to be sure she'd learned everything.

She and her husband wanted a better education for their children, so while she stayed home and ran the farm, he took petitions to several small communities and initiated construction of the first consolidated school in the county.

She tended the sick during the great influenza epidemic in 1918 and an outbreak of typhoid fever in the '20's. The local doctor would often ask her to help him deliver babies for those who could not afford to pay, because she never accepted money for her efforts.

She sewed all her family's clothes, cutting her patterns out of newspapers. She grew a big garden and canned most of their food. She dried fruit, beans and peas. She made lye soap, rendered lard and

Sylvia Brantley's mother, like woman in this photo, was a woman who believed in getting things done—like a winter's worth of canning!

utilized all of the hog by making headcheese and mincemeat from scraps. She pressed clothes with irons heated on a wood stove.

She raised ducks and used the feathers to make pillows and feather beds. Each daughter had a feather bed and two pillows in her hope chest.

On winter nights, the family would gather around the big fireplace. And by the light of a kerosene lamp, she'd give each of her children a spelling book and have them spell words aloud while she carded batts for her quilt fillers. They always excelled in spelling because they learned not only their own words, but those the other children learned as well.

As her family grew, so did those of her brothers and sisters, and she would have annual family reunions—joyous occasions for everyone to be together. She and her family helped establish and build the first church in the community, and she always hosted the visiting preacher.

No, she wasn't rich or famous, but she was a part of the building of our state, Oklahoma. How do I know this woman so well? She was my mother, Ann Dew Haines. —*Sylvia Brantley, Ada, Oklahoma*

I was born in 1935 on a farm in the middle of a pine timber belt in deep East Texas, near a place called Chireno. On the day I arrived, Daddy was extremely busy trying to get his large herd of cattle through a vat of "dip" intended to kill fever ticks.

Daddy no doubt dreamed of a boy who would grow up to be a much-needed farmhand. But life sometimes gives us things we don't expect, although in time, I became a good farmhand. I learned to take care of livestock: cattle, horses, mules, pigs, goats and fowl of all kinds. I learned to ride a horse so well that I could ride without a saddle or bridle, or stay on a horse all day if required.

I also learned how to work the fields with a mule-drawn plow. I could also hitch a team to a wagon and drive to town for supplies or take a bale of cotton to the gin. In summer, I helped cut hay, haul it to the barn and stack it.

Our farm was large and our family raised nearly all the food we needed—plenty of homegrown vegetables, fruits, meat, sweet potatoes, sugarcane, hickory nuts, pecans, black walnuts and so much more.

My love for the farm was passed down from a long line of people who had always made their livelihood off the land. My great-grandfather arrived in Texas in 1837 from Georgia. He was drawn here by the tall pine trees, the virgin soil, good clear streams and plenty of wild game.

My grandfather kept the same farm going for years and my father also had the love of the land in his blood. He added many acres of land to our farm in his lifetime.

My childhood was happy; we never really missed what we didn't have. With no electricity, our summer nights were spent on the front porch, talking to neighbors, catching fireflies and making homemade ice cream in a hand-cranked freezer. Wintertime found us in front of the woodburning fireplace, eating parched peanuts, making syrup candy and telling stories.

Five generations of our family have enjoyed the good times and weathered the hard times on this farm. Today we have nieces and nephews who come from the cities to enjoy seeing fat cattle graze and to wade barefoot in the streams. I feel that we've taken care of this farm as a legacy for the future.

—*Willie Thorp, Chireno, Texas*

My beloved grandmother, Rosine "Rosa" Margaretha Blankenhorn Weber, greatly influenced my life. My parents lived on a farm with her, so during my first 10 years, I was very much under her guidance.

Grandma spoke only German, so I first learned to speak German and then was taught English. I learned the stories of Jesus and my nursery rhymes at her knee. Eventually, she became crippled by arthritis. But she never complained and would do much work in the house and outside, either using

a cane or pushing a backless chair in front of her.

Hard work was her life. She raised six children and ran an 880-acre farm after losing two husbands. She never said, "I can't do this"; her determination taught me that a person can accomplish anything they set their mind to do. I learned compassion for others less fortunate by seeing her kindness and willingness to help.

She loved her family very much, and you could see the love they in turn felt for this wonderful lady. She was the head of the family and not one person doubted her or questioned her decisions. She kissed away the scrapes and scratches of growing up and made them all right. She helped dress dolls and told wonderful stories of faraway places and times.

I know my love for the outdoors and animals came from her teachings. I liked to help with chores, herd cattle and walk in the pasture. I saw the wonderful new things that happened each spring—a rebirth after a hard winter. To walk around in the early mornings and hear the birds singing, pheasants calling their mates and the mother cows calling their calves was like being with God when He put all living things on earth.

One spring day, my mother took my sister and me home from school. She didn't tell us why. But when we got home, all my aunts and uncles were there, talking in whispers. My aunt took us one at a time to Grandmother's bedside to say good-bye.

I sat beside her and she hugged me, kissed my cheek and told me to be a good girl because she was going to go on a journey and live with God. I knew she would always be with me because I loved her so much. But I also knew I would miss brushing her silky gray hair at night and sharing an or-

Grandmother like the one above was a strong influence in Barbara Weber Hunt's life.

ange candy slice in her room. For a 10-year-old, this was such a loss.

Now I'm an adult with four children of my own. I raised them mostly by myself. Had it not been for the strong influence of my grandmother, I know their lives would have been much different. Thanks to her, I had the determination to raise them to be good citizens. I'm very proud of my children, and I hope I've given them some of their great-grandmother's strength and ideals.

—*Barbara Weber Hunt, Bennet, Nebraska*

My brother Leroy, who is 12-1/2 years my senior, personifies country. When I was growing up on our farm 2 miles west of town, I turned to him for help, understanding and moral support.

If I needed help filling up the woodbox, he was there to bring in an armful for me. If I couldn't catch a young rooster my mother was waiting for, he'd lend a hand. And he'd often help me find that hidden hen's nest in the hayloft. And whenever he ran an errand to town, he always brought me 5¢ worth of penny candy in a paper bag.

After coming in from hunting, he'd put me on his knee and explain all about the little animals that asked for me. When I was about 6 or 8, he let me go rabbit hunting with him one evening. He even allowed me to wear the headlight for a while. I'm

Older brothers were loads of fun for their younger sisters. Here is Martin Miller and sister Diane Taylor, who sent the photo from Palmdale, California.

sure Mother was never aware of that!

I'm sure his patience must have been stretched thin on plenty of occasions. He taught me how to drive the tractor—and later the family car—on little-traveled backroads. He was the one who showed me how to skin a squirrel so that the hair wouldn't adhere to the meat. I turned to him for help in finding the perfect Christmas tree. We'd walk miles—or so it seemed—then bring it home and set it up.

Leroy was also quite the prankster. One Christmas, one of our brothers asked for new boots. Leroy put Daddy's muddy pair under the tree and told our brother that Santa's sleigh must have bogged down and he had to use the boots. Leroy also dropped fresh fruit and nuts leading up to the house, then helped me find the goodies the next morning, saying they had fallen off Santa's sleigh.

He now has grandchildren and one great-grandchild. I'm sure they have heard many stories!

—*Wilma Meister, Louin, Mississippi*

I grew up on a cotton farm in the tiny Texas panhandle town of Newlin. Daddy had quite a few acres of land and was very particular about his farming. He worked hard at building, plowing and curving the terraces and rows. It seemed incredible that one man and a tractor could carve such an intricate network out of that red earth. But he did, year after year.

Then, when the cotton stalks were covered with bright green leaves, it seemed as though the earth—until now so silent and still—had at last come to life. The green bolls appeared, turned brown and split open to reveal the soft white tufts of cotton. Sometimes travelers would stop along the highway to pull a cotton boll from our field. I guess everyone likes to have something straight from the earth.

Daddy died in January of 1993. A few weeks after the funeral, my aunt sent me a note, saying she wouldn't be surprised if Daddy had a little farm to tend in Heaven. I wouldn't be surprised, either.

—*Lynn Buchanan, Mountainburg, Arkansas*

My dad had been a lumberjack for 7 years when a land office official in Wausau asked him if he'd like to homestead in Wisconsin. Most people thought that all the land in Wisconsin had been taken years before, but a correction in land titles in 1915 turned up 160 unclaimed acres in Adams County.

Dad caught a train to Oxford, then walked the rest of the way to Jackson Township, where the land was located. He was excited when he saw the land—it was covered with trees and contained three lakes. He immediately headed back north and filed for the homestead.

The Wisconsin homestead was a lucky break for Dad, whose plans to do the same in Montana or the Dakotas failed because prices were too high. He quickly bought enough lumber to build a small shanty, then rented space in a boxcar and journeyed to Oxford by way of the Northwestern Railroad, armed with a stove, a couch, a chair, bedding and some dishes—gifts from his parents.

Upon arriving in Oxford, he took a room at the Oxford Hotel, where they let him store his furniture in a barn. He had no horse, so he walked the 10 miles to his claim every morning, then back to the hotel at night. When the shanty was completed, he paid three farmers $3 each to help him move his furnishings.

To obtain the land, the law required Dad to clear 20 acres, build a shanty, live there 6 months of the year and prove he could make a living. It wasn't easy. His first crop of corn froze on July 31, but fortunately he made money on some rutabagas.

After settling into his little two-room shanty, he built a granary, a corncrib, and a small barn to house a team of horses and two cows. He built a big barn in 1928 and eventually added 200 more acres to his farm.

There were many rough times—runaway horses, brutal winters, building a 1-1/4-mile-long road to his property, cutting wood, moving rocks, coping with fluctuating prices for hogs and milk—and, of course, the Depression. But somehow, he made it through.

Dad was the son of German immigrants who had settled just outside of Oshkosh. He was the seventh son, born on the seventh day of the seventh month in 1887. While he worked with his hands much of his life, he was also a very literate man who often recited poems or sayings for us. He was a great orator and loved quoting Shakespeare and other famous authors.

My dad met my mom in the little Davis Corners Church. They were married in 1921 and had five children—three boys and two girls. The house was small with no luxuries—not even electricity until the 1940's. But no home had more love, care and happiness.

This photo shows David Lehman's parents, Addison and Malinda, and two of his sisters, Alda and Ethel, in 1906. Like homesteader in story at left, the Lehmans had to be tough.

Dad became a pillar in our community, serving as township clerk for 12 years and Sunday school superintendent for 30 years. He also served on the Davis Corners School Board and, in his later years, was chaplain of four different senior citizen clubs. He lived for 98 years. We loved him dearly and have only happy memories of our life with him. He lived a rich, full life and we were always proud of him. —*Faith Fell, Oshkosh, Wisconsin*

My younger sister and I were the babies of our farm family and, as such, our older brothers and sisters did more of the farm chores than we did. We had some responsibilities, but mostly we played or served as everyone's little "gofers".

We were constantly together, even while sleeping. And we liked to sleep late. During the school year, Mom would wake us up before she went to the barn to help with chores. Then, worried that we weren't getting up, she'd interrupt her chores and come in and call us again. This became a habit, and she finally got frustrated enough that she decided to teach us a lesson.

One morning when the weather was still warm, she only called us once. Well, we went right back to sleep. When we finally woke up, the bus had come and gone. She had this funny look on her face—a mixture of annoyance and amusement. We were informed that we would eat our breakfast and then walk the 2 miles to school. We were angry but offered no protest because we had no grounds. We did learn our lesson!

And then there was Dad, who, having lived through the Great Depression, appeared to be a distant, stern and very conservative man. We lived on a tight budget, and Mom could only buy groceries and supplies with the check we got from selling our eggs. Fortunately, we received lots of clothing from our city relatives. Mom also baked and canned as much as possible.

But Dad had a soft side, too. One Sunday morning after church services, I was with Mom as she got her week's supply of groceries at the general store near our church. While she was purchasing school supplies for my older siblings, I begged and pleaded for a pencil and tablet of my own.

She finally relented, and I got my penny pencil and nickel tablet. I carried my little treasures most of the day. But when company came over that evening, I left my tablet and pencil under the corncrib at the hog barn. By the time our visitors left, it was raining outside—and almost as hard inside as I cried inconsolably.

It must have struck a soft spot in my father. He lit a lantern and threw a coat over his head and another over mine. He took my hand and told me to show him where the pencil and tablet were. We found them, slightly dampened, but still intact.

Both of these incidents happened about a half century ago, but I still remember them vividly. I feel they're imprinted there to remind me that both parents loved me in their own way!

—*Mary Hemmelgarn, Portland, Indiana*

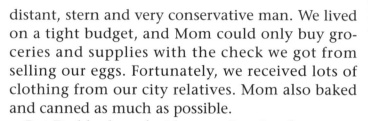

Large families provided lots of helping hands—and playmates. Photo sent by Athla Tankersley (far right) of Cheyenne, Wyoming. Her brothers and sisters in photo are, from left: Sarah Louise, Wendell, Helen, Dorothea, and Maxine.

Growing up in the country in central Georgia during the 1960's was both fun and hard work. My father was a sharecropper all of his teen and

More often than not, helping out with seasonal chores was a family affair.

adult years. My mother, in turn, was the best wife, mother, doctor, seamstress, cook and farmer that ever lived.

Some of my best memories are of her writing a grocery list on Saturday mornings and Daddy going to buy them in the town of Dexter, about 3 miles away. We couldn't wait for him to return to see if he had included a special treat.

My father's mother lived with my parents from the day they were married. She died when I was 12 years old. I have three brothers and one sister, all older than me. There's not enough paper in the world to tell the valuable things I learned living with these seven people.

Some of my most treasured memories are of everyone sitting on the front porch after supper. We'd watch for shooting stars, chase fireflies, play ball or just look at the "man in the moon". Daddy would often play the harmonica and tell us stories about his younger days. He even wrote his own songs, and we heard them all day long. He might not have made it in Nashville, but the songs certainly found a resting place in our hearts. I find myself singing these songs quite often.

He's gone now, and the old home where I grew up has been torn down; in its place stands a new house. But the old barn still exists, along with some trees under which we used to play. When I married, I only moved 8 miles away. So every time I go by our old place, I find myself slowing down—and often wiping away tears.

I can still see the house, the people sitting on the porch and the kids playing in the neatly swept (not raked!) yard or doodling for doodlebugs under the house.　　　*—Reda Rowland, Chester, Georgia*

I was born in 1925 and grew up during the Great Depression. My father, a coal miner in Montcoal, West Virginia, was severely injured on the job and couldn't work in the mines anymore. At the same time, my mother was recovering from a near-fatal case of typhoid fever contracted from contaminated well water.

So my grandfather helped our small family by allowing us to move to the hilltop part of his farm near Clendenin. My dad repaid him by helping with farm work. Both my parents continued to endure

Ottis Dilworth remembers his parents, William and Manzy (right), as hardworking folks who cared deeply about their family—and others. This photo is from 1946.

health problems, so we had a hard time making ends meet. But Dad earned what he could by helping other farmers when he was able.

My mother canned fruits and vegetables from our large garden, and we had a cow for milk and butter and pigs and chickens for meat. We added to our meat supply by hunting for rabbits and squirrels.

Each fall around Thanksgiving—when it was cold enough to keep meat, since we had no refrigerator—we'd butcher a hog for our winter meat supply. Although we were extremely poor, we had neighbors even worse off. So my dad always had me carry the hog's head to one of these neighbors who needed the meat more than we did.   —*Ottis Dilworth*
Clendenin, West Virginia

My great-grandfather, Herbert Stedman Sr., bought a farm in northern Wisconsin in 1858, and since then it has been farmed by four generations of Stedmans.

Herbert was an industrious man. He built a sawmill on the farm. He bought land, logged it and then sold it for cropland—in addition to running his dairy farm. He dammed up the river that flows through the farm and used its water to power his gristmill.

At one time, he also had a meat route. He butchered the animals he raised—pigs, cows, sheep and chickens—and sold the meat to customers in town. Because there were no refrigerators, he built a meat house over the spring down by the river to keep the meat cool.

When bricks were needed for a new schoolhouse, he got the contract; he had the only kiln in the township. The schoolhouse is now over 100 years old—the 4-H club uses it for their meetings since the kids are bused to town these days. Three generations of Stedmans attended eight grades in that building.

Herbert also made the bricks for a barn on one of his farms, and that building is still being used, even though it's 105 years old.
—*Clydene Stedman, Waupaca, Wisconsin*

One of the saddest days of our lives occurred in July of 1991. After 56 years in the dairy and cash crop business, we were forced to sell our 200 cows due to rising costs and low milk prices.

Our family farm was started by my grandfather, who arrived at Ellis Island in 1895 with 50¢ in his pocket to start his new life. He was sponsored by a Welsh community in upstate New York, where he settled and raised a family of two girls and five boys.

From this meager beginning came several farms owned by his sons and their sons. My dad was his third son and loved the farming life, so selling the herd was a bitter pill. All we could think of was the death of the farm and that way of living.

But now, 4 years later, we are starting a new venture. We just couldn't let the farm sit idle, and we missed the sight of crops growing and the sound of animals.

The pet sheep my daughter raised were the beginning. She suggested that we spin the wool ourselves. So we began washing it, combing it and spinning it on a wheel. I knit things from the spun yarn, and we've sold our finished products.

Then my son decided to use the land again and began raising organic vegetables in the pastures that didn't contain any chemicals. The first year, we sold the organic vegetables from a hay wagon by the road. We found a great demand for organic products in our community.

The second year, we all decided it was time to start working on the buildings, so we started cleaning and painting the old cow barn. Now our milk house has become an organic store with a cooler that keeps the products fresh and crisp.

What a wonderful feeling it is to see the place come alive again in new and useful ways! Maybe the cows are gone, but at least there is activity. A new generation is starting a new life on the farm.

—Barbara Couture, New Hartford, New York

I remember back when I was growing up in a farm family. I was a girl in a family of seven children—five girls and two boys. My dad's father gave him 100 acres of land when he was married, and it was all in timber. Dad worked to clear it, killing 15 rattlesnakes in the process.

All seven of us were born in the four-room house that he built. We had lots of enjoyable times living on the farm. In later years, we had a big orchard and would make apple cider in the fall. Another special time that the whole family enjoyed in autumn was when we made molasses from our own cane.

Dad also liked to grow watermelons. He had lots of melons with good yellow meat—they were my favorite. I'll never forget one time in the fall before the frost when he let me go with him to the watermelon patch. We broke some open and ate the hearts. Boy, they tasted good! We took the largest ones to the house and stored them under the bed, where they'd keep for a long time.

Being raised on a farm was the best thing that could have happened to us because we learned what it's like to live without electricity, indoor plumbing and all the modern things we have today. It made us appreciate the better things in life. I'll always remember the fun we had.

—Verna Hanning
Lynchburg, Missouri

Working together as a family made chores go that much faster—and more enjoyable, too!

Julie Habel

There's nothing like a hunk of watermelon on a hot summer day as kids (above) will attest; opposite page, clockwise from top left: curious kids look for adventure in old barn; sharing a tender moment on the farm; another way to make a summer day cooler; kids 'n piglets are a great combination; family and friends while away a summer afternoon playing cards.

157

Julie Habel

Don Condon

Stephen R. Swinburne

Farm family fun includes some horsin' around (above); continuing clockwise: birthday party blowout; kids 'n critters; hamming it up at a family gathering.

Don Condon

Threshing crew gobbles down dinner
(above); continuing clockwise: baking
cookies is almost as fun as eating them;
a quiet moment between friends on Iowa
farm; farm couple shares loving moment.

Terry Donnelly

G. Alan Nelson; inset, Ken Karlewicz

Setting sun silhouettes towering silos in Ogle County, Illinois (far left); continuing clockwise: placid farm in Defiance County, Ohio; grain wagons await corn in Bureau County, Illinois; farm outside West Arlington, Vermont; friendly cow mooves over to greet visitor.

Terry Donnelly

Ken Karlewicz

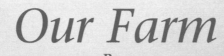

Our Farm

By
Viola Mae Baker Rippeon
Woodsboro, Maryland

God took a piece of Heaven
and gently put it down.
On part He sowed the green, green grass,
and part He made just ground.
He planted trees of different kinds
and flowers with fragrance sweet.
In the meadows He placed a stream
to make our farm complete.

He made the soil so fertile;
it grows our corn and grain.
He directs sunshine to our land;
He also sends the rain.
He watches o'er our animals—
the chickens, pigs and cows.
He's always here to guide us;
I feel His presence now.

He put us here to toil and play;
He knows our every deed.
He gives us comfort as we work;
He helps us to succeed.
We're never far from His sight;
to us will fall no harm.
This is a bit of Heaven on Earth;
we deeply love our farm.